Spelling
Handbook

k12

Book Staff and Contributors

Marianne Murphy   *Content Specialist*
David Shireman   *Instructional Designer*
Mary Beck Desmond   *Senior Text Editor*
Ron Stanley   *Text Editor*
Suzanne Montazer   *Creative Director, Print and ePublishing*
Sasha Blanton   *Senior Print Visual Designer*
Julie Jankowski, Eric Trott   *Print Visual Designers*
Stephanie Williams   *Cover Designer*
Amy Eward   *Senior Manager, Writers*
Susan Raley   *Manager, Editors*
Seth Herz   *Director, Program Management Grades K–8*

Maria Szalay   *Senior Vice President, Product Development*
John Holdren   *Senior Vice President, Content and Curriculum*
David Pelizzari   *Vice President, Content and Curriculum*
Kim Barcas   *Vice President, Creative*
Laura Seuschek   *Vice President, Instructional Design and Evaluation & Research*
Aaron Hall   *Vice President, Program Management*

Lisa Dimaio Iekel   *Production Manager*
John Agnone   *Director of Publications*

About K12 Inc.

K12 Inc., a technology-based education company, is the nation's leading provider of proprietary curriculum and online education programs to students in grades K–12. K^{12} provides its curriculum and academic services to online schools, traditional classrooms, blended school programs, and directly to families. K12 Inc. also operates the K^{12} International Academy, an accredited, diploma-granting online private school serving students worldwide. K^{12}'s mission is to provide any child the curriculum and tools to maximize success in life, regardless of geographic, financial, or demographic circumstances. K12 Inc. is accredited by CITA. More information can be found at www.K12.com.

978-1-60153-171-1
Printed by RR Donnelley & Sons, Roanoke, VA, USA, May 2015

Contents

K¹² Spelling Course Overview

Overview

My spelling is Wobbly. It's good spelling but it Wobbles, and the letters get in the wrong places. — A. A. MILNE

The goal of K¹² Spelling is to ensure students don't wobble with their spelling the way Winnie-the-Pooh does. As an engaging, portable program that can be tailored to the individual needs of students, K¹² Spelling will help students master the conventions of spelling needed to be proficient readers and writers.

While many may wonder about the need for formal spelling instruction in the digital age, K¹² firmly believes in the power and necessity of mastering the traditional subject of spelling. K¹² Spelling focuses on learning to recognize patterns rather than memorizing rules—no spelling rule is 100 percent reliable. Research shows that good readers and spellers do not decode (read) and encode (spell) rules, but rather letter patterns that help them identify words and differentiate one word from another.

A great deal of research shows that continually revisiting and building on mastered concepts helps students master new concepts. With each subsequent grade level, spelling conventions build on previously mastered content while giving students many options for multimodal learning. Throughout grades 1–5, students build a strong foundation that leads to a strong storehouse of knowledge about spelling and the English language.

K¹² Spelling is designed to accommodate students who will master the content at different paces and who will require varying amounts of study. K¹² believes that students can learn to spell words quickly by studying spelling patterns that are common to many words. A certain number of common words fall outside these conventions, and students need to learn to spell those words quickly in preparation for the demands of grade-level writing requirements.

To balance the goals of learning to spell both within and outside spelling conventions, the spelling words in K¹² Spelling are divided into four categories: Heart Words, Target Words, Challenge Words, and Alternate Words.

Heart Words represent some of the most commonly spelled words outside the spelling conventions taught at each grade level. Other programs may refer to these as sight words, trick words, or snap words. Heart Words do not follow the spelling patterns being covered in the unit, but it is important for students to learn to spell these very common words that have to be learned "by heart." A unit will typically include two to four Heart Words. You will help students track which Heart Words they have mastered, and students will continue to study each Heart Word until they have mastered it. All students are expected to demonstrate mastery of Heart Words.

Target Words follow the spelling pattern being studied in a unit. For example, all Target Words for a given unit may be words that end with a double letter. Along with the Heart Words, these words represent the core content to be learned by students in a unit. A unit will present ten Target Words. All students are expected to demonstrate mastery of Target Words.

Challenge Words also follow the spelling convention being studied in any given unit, but are somewhat more difficult to spell. Challenge Words will be presented to students only if they first show mastery of the unit's Heart Words and Target Words. Each unit includes two to four Challenge Words. Not all students are expected to demonstrate mastery of Challenge Words.

Alternate Words are like Target Words and represent another set of words that follow the spelling convention being studied in the unit. Alternate Words are a source of extra words for students who show ready mastery of the Heart Words and Target Words. Ten Alternate Words are identified in most units. Not all students are expected to demonstrate mastery of Alternate Words.

Unit Plans

K[12] Spelling presents a cohesive, pattern-based program designed to enable you to guide students through the instruction of these four different types of words.

K[12] Spelling Purple consists of 36 units. Each five-day unit focuses on a particular spelling convention and follows a set, repeated pattern.

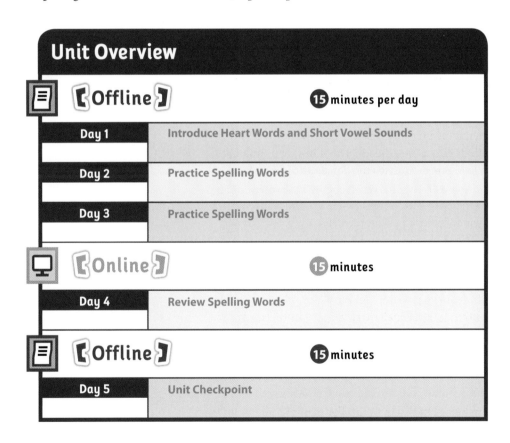

Unit Overview

❮Offline❯   **15** minutes per day

Day 1	Introduce Heart Words and Short Vowel Sounds
Day 2	Practice Spelling Words
Day 3	Practice Spelling Words

❮Online❯   **15** minutes

| Day 4 | Review Spelling Words |

❮Offline❯   **15** minutes

| Day 5 | Unit Checkpoint |

Day 1

On Day 1, students' spelling list, or Words to Learn, is determined. Students will take a pretest, establishing their initial level of mastery of the spelling words presented in that unit. You will then guide students through the discovery of the spelling convention being studied in that unit, and students will briefly practice the spelling words that they did not master in the pretest.

Day 2

You will use the Activity Bank to practice spelling words with students. The Activity Bank is a collection of interactive, offline activities designed to allow students to practice spelling words in a variety of ways. You can choose any of the activities in the Activity Bank to do on Days 2 and 3 of the unit, so try out as many of the activities as possible to discover which ones motivate and produce the best learning for your students.

Day 3

You will use the Activity Bank to practice spelling words with students. You are encouraged, but not required, to choose activities different from those you used on Day 2.

Day 4

Students will play an online game in which they review the spelling words in the unit. At the beginning of the game, you will choose whether the game should present only the Heart Words and Target Words to students, or whether Challenge Words or Alternate Words should also be included. This online review serves as preparation for the assessment (Unit Checkpoint) on Day 5.

Day 5

Students will complete an offline Unit Checkpoint covering the Heart Words and Target Words from the unit. Only the Heart Words and Target Words are assessed because they represent the core content of the course. You will enter the results of the assessment online to track student progress.

Since each unit follows the same pattern, full activity directions for each day will be repeated only in the first two Unit Plans. In subsequent units, an abbreviated version of the instructions is presented. However, the spelling words, materials lists, advance preparation, and any guidance particular to a unit will be presented in each specific Unit Plan.

Review Units

Every sixth unit in K[12] Spelling is a review unit. Review units consist of the same introduction, practice, and assessment procedures as other units. But instead of introducing a new spelling convention, they review the spelling conventions studied in the previous five units. In the review unit, all the Heart Words from the previous five units are presented, and the Target Words are made up of a selection of words from previous units representing each of the spelling conventions covered. The Challenge Words and Alternate Words are new words that also represent the spelling conventions studied in the previous five units.

Spelling

Handbook

Heart Words and Digraphs (A)

Target spelling convention – **two letters that combine to make a single sound**

When a single sound is spelled with two letters, we call these letters a digraph. This unit's Target Words all contain digraphs.

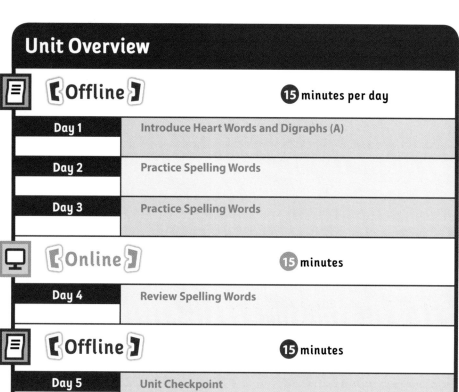

Unit Overview

📋 **⟨ Offline ⟩** 🕐 15 minutes per day

Day 1	Introduce Heart Words and Digraphs (A)
Day 2	Practice Spelling Words
Day 3	Practice Spelling Words

🖥️ **⟨ Online ⟩** 🕐 15 minutes

Day 4	Review Spelling Words

📋 **⟨ Offline ⟩** 🕐 15 minutes

Day 5	Unit Checkpoint

🤍 **Heart Words** ············

from   does

⭐ **Challenge Words** ············

thermal   within   relish

◎ **Target Words** ············

lock	chin	this
dish	shop	whip
than	that	which
back		

Alternate Words ············

with	cash	mock
wish	ship	math
dock	mash	bath
chop		

【 Offline 】 ⑮ minutes per day

Complete the Spelling activities with students.

Day 1

Introduce Heart Words and Digraphs (A)

【 Materials 】

- index cards (25)
- whiteboard (optional)

Advance Preparation

Write each Heart, Target, Challenge, and Alternate Word on a separate index card. Use small symbols or letters to indicate which type of word is written on each card. For example, you can use a T for Target Words, a heart symbol for Heart Words, a C for Challenge Words, and an A for Alternate Words.

| T shop | ♡ a | C suntan | A dock |

Pretest

1. Using the index cards you prepared, **say** each Heart and Target Word and have students write it on a whiteboard or sheet of paper. As you give the pretest, place the cards for words students spelled correctly in a Mastered pile. Place the cards for words students misspelled in a Words to Learn pile.

2. **Gather** the cards for all the words students have misspelled, which will be students' Words to Learn for this unit. It is best if students have between 10 and 20 Words to Learn, depending on students' rate of mastery.

   ▸ If students misspelled only a few words, consider adding a few Alternate or Challenge Words.
   ▸ If students didn't misspell any Heart or Target Words, give them a pretest using the Alternate and Challenge Words. Add the words they misspell to their Words to Learn.

Note: If students didn't misspell any Heart, Target, Challenge, or Alternate Words, mark Lessons 2 and 3 complete and move to the online activity for Day 4 to practice for the Unit Checkpoint on Day 5.

Heart Words

Heart Words do not follow spelling conventions, so we learn them "by heart."

⟳ *Skip this activity if students didn't misspell any Heart Words on this unit's pretest.*

1. **Gather** the Words to Learn cards for any Heart Words.

2. **Practice** the Heart Words.

   ▸ Have students choose a card and read the word aloud.

      Successful?
      • Cover the card and have students write it on a whiteboard or sheet of paper.
      • Go to the next word.

      Not successful?
      • Say the word and have students spell it aloud.
      • Have students picture the letters of the word in their mind.
      • Have students write the word on a whiteboard or sheet of paper.
      • Have students spell the word aloud again.

   ▸ Continue this way through all the new Heart Words for this unit.

3. **Track mastery** of Heart Words.

   ▸ When students read and spell a Heart Word correctly, mark the index card with the date.
   ▸ When any index card has three dates marked on it, that card should be moved from the group of Heart Words students are still working on to the group of Heart Words students have mastered.

Target Words

Target Words have the single spelling convention we're focusing on in this lesson.

⟳ *Skip this activity if students didn't misspell any Target Words on this unit's pretest.*

1. **Gather** the Words to Learn cards for any Target Words.

2. **Discover** the new spelling convention.

   ▸ Explain the new spelling convention described at the beginning of this unit.
   ▸ Have students search for the new spelling convention in the words on the index cards.
   ▸ Say aloud and discuss the new spelling convention in each Target Word.
   ▸ Ask students to picture the letters of the word in their mind.

3. **Practice** the Target Words.

   ▸ Have students sound out the Target Words.
   ▸ Have students point out the spelling convention in the words.
   ▸ Say a word and have students spell it aloud.

• Go to the next word.

• Review the correct spelling with students.
• Have students write the word on a whiteboard or sheet of paper.
• Have students spell the word aloud again.

▸ Continue this way through all the Target Words for this unit.

Challenge Words

Challenge Words follow the unit's spelling convention, but are more difficult than the Target Words.

⟲ *Skip this activity if students are struggling with the Heart Words and Target Words.*

1. **Gather** the Words to Learn cards for any Challenge Words.

2. **Discover** the new spelling convention in the Challenge Words.

 ▸ Explain the new spelling convention described at the beginning of this unit.
 ▸ Have students search for the new spelling convention in the words on the index cards.
 ▸ Say each word and have students spell it aloud.
 ▸ Have students picture the letters of each word in their mind.

3. **Practice** the Challenge Words.

 ▸ Have students write the word on a whiteboard or sheet of paper.
 ▸ Have students spell the word aloud again.

Alternate Words

Alternate Words follow the unit's spelling convention.

⟲ *Skip this activity if students don't have any Words to Learn cards for Alternate Words.*

1. **Gather** the Words to Learn cards for any Alternate Words.

2. **Discover** the new spelling convention in the Alternate Words.

 ▸ Explain the new spelling convention described at the beginning of this unit.
 ▸ Have students search for the new spelling convention in the words on the index cards.
 ▸ Say each word and have students spell it aloud.
 ▸ Have students picture the letters of each word in their mind.

3. **Practice** the Alternate Words.

 ▸ Have students write the word on a whiteboard or sheet of paper.
 ▸ Have students spell the word aloud again.

Day 2 ....

Practice Spelling Words

Students need to practice only the words on their Words to Learn cards from Day 1.

1. **Choose** a spelling activity from the Activity Bank on pages **SP 150–157**.

2. **Use *all*** the Words to Learn during the activity.

3. **Choose** a second activity if you have time.

Day 3 ....

Practice Spelling Words

Follow the same procedure as on Day 2, but choose different activities from the Activity Bank.

 **15 minutes**

Day 4 ....

Review Spelling Words

Help students **find the online review activity**, choose Challenge Words or Alternate Words if students have studied those words in this unit, and provide support as needed.

[Offline] ⏱ 15 minutes

Day 5

Unit Checkpoint

Students will complete an offline Unit Checkpoint covering the Heart Words and Target Words from the unit. (Challenge Words and Alternate Words are not included on the Checkpoint.)

1. **Dictate** the Heart Words and Target Words.

   ▸ Have students write the words on a sheet of paper.

2. **Check** students' answers.

   ▸ Circle the words students spell incorrectly.
   ▸ Enter students' results online.

3. **Review** the words students misspelled.

   ▸ Gather these Words to Learn cards and put them aside for further practice as time allows.

Rewards:

• If students scored 80 percent or above on the Unit Checkpoint, add a sticker to the Unit 1 box on students' My Accomplishments chart. If students scored under 80 percent, continue to practice the words that they missed and add a sticker to this unit once they have mastered the words.

• Help students find and play the online Spelling game, Spell 'n' Stack. Students should use level 1.

Heart Words and Digraphs (B)

Target spelling convention – **two letters that combine to make a single sound**

When a single sound is spelled with two letters, we call these letters digraphs. This unit's Target Words all contain digraphs.

Objectives
- Spell Heart Words.
- Spell words containing the digraphs *ck, sh, th, ch,* or *wh.*

Unit Overview

📄 〖Offline〗 ⏱ 15 minutes per day

Day 1	Introduce Heart Words and Digraphs (B)
Day 2	Practice Spelling Words
Day 3	Practice Spelling Words

💻 〖Online〗 ⏱ 15 minutes

| Day 4 | Review Spelling Words |

📄 〖Offline〗 ⏱ 15 minutes

| Day 5 | Unit Checkpoint |

❤ Heart Words

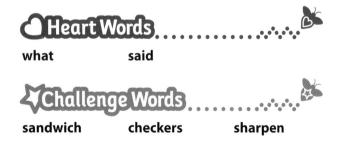

what   said

⭐ Challenge Words

sandwich   checkers   sharpen

◎ Target Words

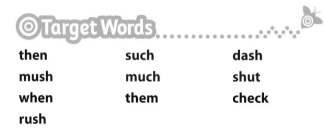

then	such	dash
mush	much	shut
when	them	check
rush		

Alternate Words

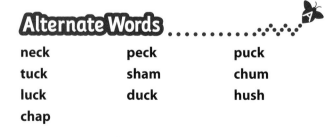

neck	peck	puck
tuck	sham	chum
luck	duck	hush
chap		

[Offline] 🕐 **minutes per day**

Complete the Spelling activities with students.

Day 1 ....

Introduce Heart Words and Digraphs (B)

[Materials]

- index cards (25)
- whiteboard (optional)

Advance Preparation

Write each Heart, Target, Challenge, and Alternate Word on a separate index card. Use small symbols or letters to indicate which type of word is written on each card. For example, you can use a T for Target Words, a heart symbol for Heart Words, a C for Challenge Words, and an A for Alternate Words.

| T shop | ♡ a | C suntan | A dock |

Pretest

1. Using the index cards you prepared, **say** each Heart and Target Word and have students write it on a whiteboard or sheet of paper. As you give the pretest, place the cards for words students spelled correctly in a Mastered pile. Place the cards for words students misspelled in a Words to Learn pile.

2. **Gather** the cards for all the words students have misspelled, which will be students' Words to Learn for this unit. It is best if students have between 10 and 20 Words to Learn, depending on students' rate of mastery.

   ▸ If students misspelled only a few words, consider adding a few Alternate or Challenge Words.
   ▸ If students didn't misspell any Heart or Target Words, give them a pretest using the Alternate and Challenge Words. Add the words they misspell to their Words to Learn.

Note: If students didn't misspell any Heart, Target, Challenge, or Alternate Words, mark Lessons 2 and 3 complete and move to the online activity for Day 4 to practice for the Unit Checkpoint on Day 5.

Heart Words

Heart Words do not follow spelling conventions, so we learn them "by heart."

⮕ *Skip this activity if students didn't misspell any Heart Words on this unit's pretest.*

1. **Gather** the Words to Learn cards for any Heart Words.

2. **Practice** the *new* Heart Words.

   ▸ Have students choose a card and read the word aloud.

   Successful?
   - Cover the card and have students write it on a whiteboard or sheet of paper.
   - Go to the next word.

   Not successful?
   - Say the word and have students spell it aloud.
   - Have students picture the letters of the word in their mind.
   - Have students write the word on a whiteboard or sheet of paper.
   - Have students spell the word aloud again.

   ▸ Continue this way through all the new Heart Words for this unit.

3. **Track mastery** of Heart Words.

   ▸ When students read and spell a Heart Word correctly, mark the index card with the date.
   ▸ When any index card has three dates marked on it, that card should be moved from the group of Heart Words students are still working on to the group of Heart Words students have mastered.

Target Words

Target Words have the single spelling convention we're focusing on in this lesson.

⮕ *Skip this activity if students didn't misspell any Target Words on this unit's pretest.*

1. **Gather** the Words to Learn cards for any Target Words.

2. **Discover** the new spelling convention.

   ▸ Explain the new spelling convention described at the beginning of this unit.
   ▸ Have students search for the new spelling convention in the words on the index cards.
   ▸ Say aloud and discuss the new spelling convention in each Target Word.
   ▸ Have students picture the letters of the word in their mind.

3. **Practice** the Target Words.

   ▸ Have students sound out the Target Words.
   ▸ Have students point out the spelling convention in the new words.
   ▸ Say a word and ask students to spell it aloud.

Successful?

- Go to the next word.

Not successful?

- Review the correct spelling with students.
- Have students write the word on a whiteboard or sheet of paper.
- Have students spell the word aloud again.

▸ Continue this way through all the Target Words for this unit.

4. **Practice** the Target Words.

▸ Have students sound out the Target Words.
▸ Have students point out the spelling convention in the words.
▸ Say a word and ask students to spell it aloud.

Successful?

- Go to the next word.

Not successful?

- Review the correct spelling with students.
- Have students write the word on a whiteboard or sheet of paper.
- Have students spell the word aloud again.

▸ Continue this way through all the Target Words for this unit.

Challenge Words

Challenge Words follow the unit's spelling convention, but are more difficult than the Target Words.

⊃ *Skip this activity if students are struggling with the Heart Words and Target Words.*

1. **Gather** the Words to Learn cards for any Challenge Words.

2. **Discover** the new spelling convention in the Challenge Words.

▸ Explain the new spelling convention described at the beginning of this unit.
▸ Have students search for the new spelling convention in the words on the index cards.
▸ Say each word and have students spell it aloud.
▸ Have students picture the letters of each word in their mind.

3. **Practice** the Challenge Words.

▸ Have students write the word on a whiteboard or sheet of paper.
▸ Ask students to spell the word aloud again.

Alternate Words

Alternate Words follow the unit's spelling convention.

⊃ *Skip this activity if students don't have any Words to Learn cards for Alternate Words.*

1. **Gather** the Words to Learn cards for any Alternate Words.

2. **Discover** the new spelling convention in the Alternate Words.

- ▸ Explain the new spelling convention described at the beginning of this unit.
- ▸ Have students search for the new spelling convention in the words on the index cards.
- ▸ Say each word and have students spell it aloud.
- ▸ Have students picture the letters of each word in their mind.

3. **Practice** the Alternate Words.

- ▸ Have students write the word on a whiteboard or sheet of paper.
- ▸ Ask students to spell the word aloud again.

Day 2

Practice Spelling Words

Students need to practice only the words on their Words to Learn cards from Day 1.

1. **Choose** a spelling activity from the Activity Bank on pages **SP 150–157**.

2. **Use *all*** the Words to Learn during the activity.

3. **Choose** a second activity if you have time.

Day 3

Practice Spelling Words

Follow the same procedure as on Day 2, but choose different activities from the Activity Bank.

 **15 minutes**

Day 4

Review Spelling Words

Help students **find the online review activity**, choose Challenge Words or Alternate Words if students have studied those words in this unit, and provide support as needed.

Offline 🕐 **15** minutes

Day 5

Unit Checkpoint

Students will complete an offline Unit Checkpoint covering the Heart Words and Target Words from the unit. (Challenge Words and Alternate Words are not included on the Checkpoint.)

1. **Dictate** the Heart Words and Target Words.

   ▶ Have students write the words on a sheet of paper.

2. **Check** students' answers.

   ▶ Circle the words students spell incorrectly.
   ▶ Enter students' results online.

3. **Review** the words students misspelled.

   ▶ Gather these Words to Learn cards and put them aside for further practice as time allows.

 Rewards:

- If students scored 80 percent or above on the Unit Checkpoint, add a sticker to the Unit 2 box on students' My Accomplishments chart. If students scored under 80 percent, continue to practice the words that they missed and add a sticker to this unit once they have mastered the words.

- Help students find and play the online Spelling game, Spell 'n' Stack. Students should use level 1.

Heart Words and Ending Blends

Target spelling convention — **consecutive consonants that retain their own sounds and conclude words**

When two or three consonants in a row each retain their own sound, we call them a blend. This unit's Target Words each end with a blend.

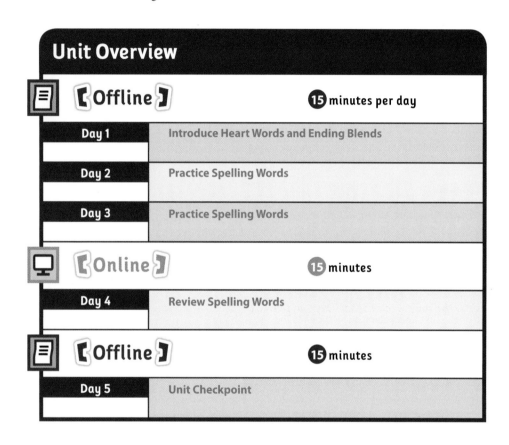

Unit Overview

Offline — 15 minutes per day

Day 1	Introduce Heart Words and Ending Blends
Day 2	Practice Spelling Words
Day 3	Practice Spelling Words

Online — 15 minutes

| Day 4 | Review Spelling Words |

Offline — 15 minutes

| Day 5 | Unit Checkpoint |

♡ Heart Words

says   front

☆ Challenge Words

defend   adrift   shrimp

◎ Target Words

hand	soft	belt
gift	bent	tent
bump	milk	fond
pond		

Alternate Words

land	jump	felt
pump	hunt	loft
lift	find	send
silk		

 **Offline** ⏱ **15** minutes per day

Complete the Spelling activities with students. **For the full instructions for each activity, refer to pages SP 8–13.**

Day 1

Introduce Heart Words and Ending Blends

Materials

- index cards (25)
- whiteboard (optional)

Advance Preparation

Write each Heart, Target, Challenge, and Alternate Word on a separate index card. Indicate on each card whether a word is a Heart, Target, Challenge, or Alternate Word.

Pretest

1. **Administer** a pretest using the Heart and Target Words.

2. **Gather** students' Words to Learn cards.

Note: If students didn't misspell any Heart, Target, Challenge, or Alternate Words, mark Lessons 2 and 3 complete and move to the online activity for Day 4 to practice for the Unit Checkpoint on Day 5.

Heart Words

⊃ *Skip this activity if students didn't misspell any Heart Words on this unit's pretest.*

1. **Gather** the Words to Learn cards for any Heart Words.

2. **Practice** the *new* Heart Words.

3. **Practice** *all* Heart Words.

4. **Track mastery** of Heart Words.

Target Words

⊃ *Skip this activity if students didn't misspell any Target Words on this unit's pretest.*

1. **Gather** the Words to Learn cards for any Target Words.

2. **Discover** the new spelling convention.

3. **Practice** the Target Words.

Challenge Words

↪ *Skip this activity if students are struggling with the Heart Words and Target Words.*

1. **Gather** the Words to Learn cards for any Challenge Words.
2. **Discover** the new spelling convention in the Challenge Words.
3. **Practice** the Challenge Words.

Alternate Words

↪ *Skip this activity if students don't have any Words to Learn cards for Alternate Words.*

1. **Gather** the Words to Learn cards for any Alternate Words.
2. **Discover** the new spelling convention in the Alternate Words.
3. **Practice** the Alternate Words.

Day 2 ···

Practice Spelling Words

Practice using the Activity Bank.

Day 3 ···

Practice Spelling Words

Practice using the Activity Bank.

 **15 minutes**

Day 4 ···

Review Spelling Words

Review using the online activity.

 **[Offline]** 🕔 **minutes**

Day 5

Unit Checkpoint

1. **Dictate** the Heart Words and Target Words.

2. **Check** students' answers.

3. **Review** the words students misspelled.

Rewards:

- If students scored 80 percent or above on the Unit Checkpoint, add a sticker to the Unit 3 box on students' My Accomplishments chart. If students scored under 80 percent, continue to practice the words that they missed and add a sticker to this unit once they have mastered the words.

- Help students find and play the online Spelling game, Spell 'n' Stack. Students should use level 1.

Heart Words and Beginning Blends

Target spelling convention – **consecutive consonants that retain their own sounds and begin words**

When two or three consonants in a row each retain their own sound, we call them a blend. This unit's Target Words each begin with a blend.

Objectives
- Spell Heart Words.
- Spell words beginning with consonant blends.

Unit Overview

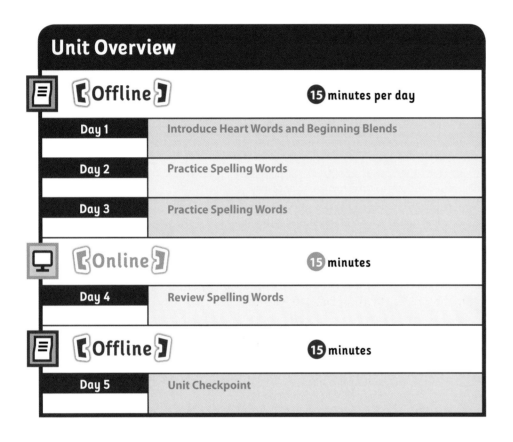

Offline   🕐 **15 minutes per day**

Day 1	Introduce Heart Words and Beginning Blends
Day 2	Practice Spelling Words
Day 3	Practice Spelling Words

Online   🕐 **15 minutes**

| Day 4 | Review Spelling Words |

Offline   🕐 **15 minutes**

| Day 5 | Unit Checkpoint |

Heart Words

won   busy

Challenge Words

travel   dragon   crunch

Target Words

spot	speck	drum
stop	swim	crab
sled	crib	splash
brush		

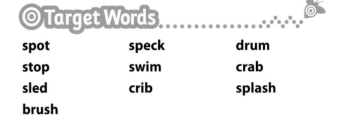

Alternate Words

trot	fled	grab
grin	brick	frog
prop	crush	crash
slip		

[Offline] ⏱ minutes per day

Complete the Spelling activities with students. **For the full instructions for each activity, refer to pages SP 8–13.**

Day 1

Introduce Heart Words and Beginning Blends

[Materials]
- index cards (25)
- whiteboard (optional)

Advance Preparation

Write each Heart, Target, Challenge, and Alternate Word on a separate index card. Indicate on each card whether a word is a Heart, Target, Challenge, or Alternate Word.

Pretest

1. **Administer** a pretest using the Heart and Target Words.

2. **Gather** students' Words to Learn cards.

Note: If students didn't misspell any Heart, Target, Challenge, or Alternate Words, mark lessons 2 and 3 complete and move to the online activity for Day 4 to practice for the Unit Checkpoint on Day 5.

Heart Words

➲ *Skip this activity if students didn't misspell any Heart Words on this unit's pretest.*

1. **Gather** the Words to Learn cards for any Heart Words.

2. **Practice** the *new* Heart Words.

3. **Practice** *all* Heart Words.

4. **Track mastery** of Heart Words.

Target Words

➲ *Skip this activity if students didn't misspell any Target Words on this unit's pretest.*

1. **Gather** the Words to Learn cards for any Target Words.

2. **Discover** the new spelling convention.

3. **Practice** the Target Words.

Challenge Words

⮑ *Skip this activity if students are struggling with the Heart Words and Target Words.*

1. **Gather** the Words to Learn cards for any Challenge Words.
2. **Discover** the new spelling convention in the Challenge Words.
3. **Practice** the Challenge Words.

Alternate Words

⮑ *Skip this activity if students don't have any Words to Learn cards for Alternate Words.*

1. **Gather** the Words to Learn cards for any Alternate Words.
2. **Discover** the new spelling convention in the Alternate Words.
3. **Practice** the Alternate Words.

Day 2 ···

Practice Spelling Words

Practice using the Activity Bank.

Day 3 ···

Practice Spelling Words

Practice using the Activity Bank.

 **15 minutes**

Day 4 ···

Review Spelling Words

Review using the online activity.

[Offline] 🕤 minutes

Day 5

Unit Checkpoint

1. **Dictate** the Heart Words and Target Words.

2. **Check** students' answers.

3. **Review** the words students misspelled.

Rewards:

- If students scored 80 percent or above on the Unit Checkpoint, add a sticker to the Unit 4 box on students' My Accomplishments chart. If students scored under 80 percent, continue to practice the words that they missed and add a sticker to this unit once they have mastered the words.

- Help students find and play the online Spelling game, Spell 'n' Stack. Students should use level 1.

Heart Words and Beginning & Ending Blends

Target spelling convention – consecutive consonants that retain their own sounds and begin or end words

When two or three consonants in a row each retain their own sound, we call them a blend. Some of this unit's Target Words begin with a blend, and some end with a blend.

Unit Overview

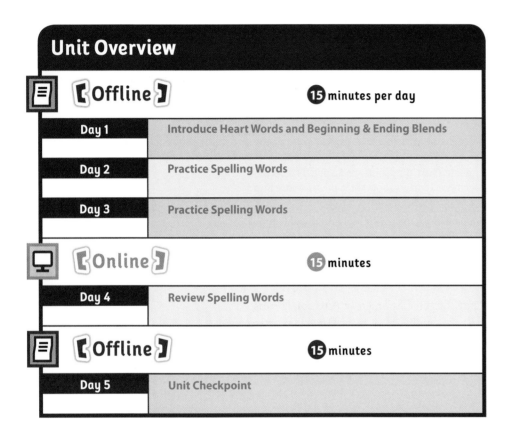

📄 【Offline】		⏱15 minutes per day
Day 1	Introduce Heart Words and Beginning & Ending Blends	
Day 2	Practice Spelling Words	
Day 3	Practice Spelling Words	

🖥 【Online】		⏱15 minutes
Day 4	Review Spelling Words	

📄 【Offline】		⏱15 minutes
Day 5	Unit Checkpoint	

☁ Heart Words

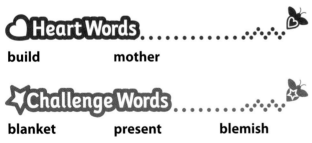

build	mother

✩ Challenge Words

blanket	present	blemish

◎ Target Words

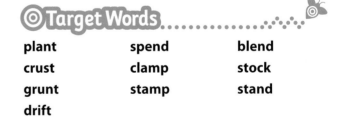

plant	spend	blend
crust	clamp	stock
grunt	stamp	stand
drift		

Alternate Words

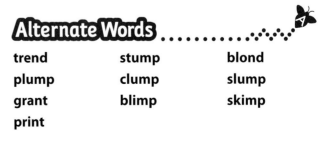

trend	stump	blond
plump	clump	slump
grant	blimp	skimp
print		

【 Offline 】 ⏱ 15 minutes per day

Complete the Spelling activities with students. **For the full instructions for each activity, refer to pages SP 8–13.**

Day 1 ....

Introduce Heart Words and Beginning & Ending Blends

【 Materials 】
- index cards (25)
- whiteboard (optional)

Advance Preparation

Write each Heart, Target, Challenge, and Alternate Word on a separate index card. Indicate on each card whether a word is a Heart, Target, Challenge, or Alternate Word.

Pretest

1. **Administer** a pretest using the Heart and Target Words.
2. **Gather** students' Words to Learn cards.

Note: If students didn't misspell any Heart, Target, Challenge, or Alternate Words, mark lessons 2 and 3 complete and move to the online activity for Day 4 to practice for the Unit Checkpoint on Day 5.

Heart Words

➲ *Skip this activity if students didn't misspell any Heart Words on this unit's pretest.*

1. **Gather** the Words to Learn cards for any Heart Words.
2. **Practice** the *new* Heart Words.
3. **Practice** *all* Heart Words.
4. **Track mastery** of Heart Words.

Target Words

➲ *Skip this activity if students didn't misspell any Target Words on this unit's pretest.*

1. **Gather** the Words to Learn cards for any Target Words.
2. **Discover** the new spelling convention.
3. **Practice** the Target Words.

Challenge Words

➲ *Skip this activity if students are struggling with the Heart Words and Target Words.*

1. **Gather** the Words to Learn cards for any Challenge Words.
2. **Discover** the new spelling convention in the Challenge Words.
3. **Practice** the Challenge Words.

Alternate Words

➲ *Skip this activity if students don't have any Words to Learn cards for Alternate Words.*

1. **Gather** the Words to Learn cards for any Alternate Words.
2. **Discover** the new spelling convention in the Alternate Words.
3. **Practice** the Alternate Words.

Day 2 ....

Practice Spelling Words

Practice using the Activity Bank.

Day 3 ....

Practice Spelling Words

Practice using the Activity Bank.

 **15 minutes**

Day 4 ....

Review Spelling Words

Review using the online activity.

Day 5

Unit Checkpoint

1. **Dictate** the Heart Words and Target Words.

2. **Check** students' answers.

3. **Review** the words students misspelled.

Rewards:

- If students scored 80 percent or above on the Unit Checkpoint, add a sticker to the Unit 5 box on students' My Accomplishments chart. If students scored under 80 percent, continue to practice the words that they missed and add a sticker to this unit once they have mastered the words.

- Help students find and play the online Spelling game, Spell 'n' Stack. Students should use level 1.

Review Heart Words, Digraphs, and Blends

In this unit, students will review the spelling conventions and Heart Words they studied in the previous five units. Refer back to the Unit Plans of previous units for a detailed description of each spelling convention.

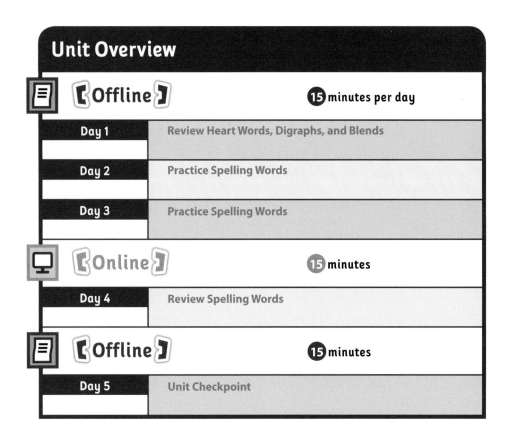

Unit Overview

Offline — 15 minutes per day

Day 1	Review Heart Words, Digraphs, and Blends
Day 2	Practice Spelling Words
Day 3	Practice Spelling Words

Online — 15 minutes

| Day 4 | Review Spelling Words |

Offline — 15 minutes

| Day 5 | Unit Checkpoint |

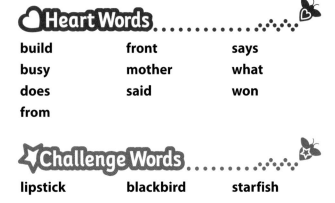

Heart Words

build	front	says
busy	mother	what
does	said	won
from		

Challenge Words

| lipstick | blackbird | starfish |

Target Words

then	swim	brush
lock	gift	much
shop	belt	plant
stop	hand	grunt
crab		

Alternate Words

| stamps | small | champ |
| belts | blend | |

[Offline] ⏱ 15 minutes per day

Complete the Spelling activities with students. **For the full instructions for each activity, refer to pages SP 8–13.**

Day 1 ....

Review Heart Words, Digraphs, and Blends

[Materials]

- index cards (8)
- whiteboard (optional)

Advance Preparation

Gather the index cards you made previously for the Heart and Target Words listed. Write each Challenge and Alternate Word on a separate index card. Indicate on each card whether a word is a Challenge or Alternate Word.

Pretest

1. **Administer** a pretest using the Heart and Target Words.

2. **Gather** students' Words to Learn cards.

Note: If students didn't misspell any Heart, Target, Challenge, or Alternate Words, mark lessons 2 and 3 complete and move to the online activity for Day 4 to practice for the Unit Checkpoint on Day 5.

Heart Words

➲ *Skip this activity if students didn't misspell any Heart Words on this unit's pretest.*

1. **Gather** the Words to Learn cards for any Heart Words.

2. **Practice** the Heart Words.

3. **Track mastery** of Heart Words.

Target Words

➲ *Skip this activity if students didn't misspell any Target Words on this unit's pretest.*

1. **Gather** the Words to Learn cards for any Target Words.

2. **Review** the previously studied spelling convention in each Target Word.

3. **Practice** the Target Words.

Challenge Words

➲ *Skip this activity if students are struggling with the Heart Words and Target Words.*

1. **Gather** the Words to Learn cards for any Challenge Words.

2. **Review** the previously studied spelling convention in each Challenge Word.

3. **Practice** the Challenge Words.

Alternate Words

➲ *Skip this activity if students don't have any Words to Learn cards for Alternate Words.*

1. **Gather** the Words to Learn cards for any Alternate Words.

2. **Review** the previously studied spelling convention in each Alternate Word.

3. **Practice** the Alternate Words.

Day 2 ....

Practice Spelling Words

Practice using the Activity Bank.

Day 3 ....

Practice Spelling Words

Practice using the Activity Bank.

 **15 minutes**

Day 4 ....

Review Spelling Words

Review using the online activity.

⟦ Offline ⟧ ⑮ minutes

Day 5

Unit Checkpoint

1. **Dictate** the Heart Words and Target Words.

2. **Check** students' answers.

3. **Review** the words students misspelled.

Rewards:

- If students scored 80 percent or above on the Unit Checkpoint, add a sticker to the Unit 6 box on students' My Accomplishments chart. If students scored under 80 percent, continue to practice the words that they missed and add a sticker to this unit once they have mastered the words.

- Help students find and play the online Spelling game, Spell 'n' Stack. Students should use level 1.

Heart Words and Double Trouble Endings

Target spelling convention — **short vowel + doubled last letter that makes one sound**

When a word ends with a short vowel and then the letters *f*, *l*, *s*, and sometimes *z*, we double the last letter. The doubled letters only make one sound. This unit's Target Words each end in a double letter.

Objectives
- Spell Heart Words.
- Spell words ending with the double letters *ss*, *zz*, *ll*, or *ff*.

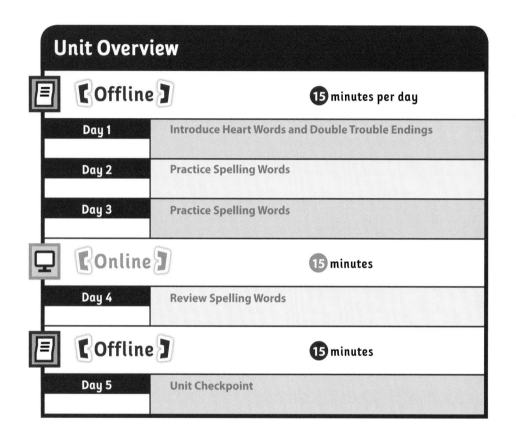

Unit Overview

Offline — 15 minutes per day

Day 1	Introduce Heart Words and Double Trouble Endings
Day 2	Practice Spelling Words
Day 3	Practice Spelling Words

Online — 15 minutes

| Day 4 | Review Spelling Words |

Offline — 15 minutes

| Day 5 | Unit Checkpoint |

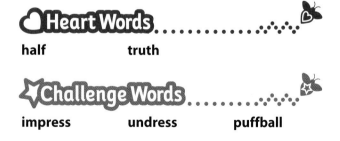

Heart Words

half	truth

Challenge Words

impress	undress	puffball

Target Words

grass	miss	dull
fizz	puff	doll
pass	cliff	dress
tell		

Alternate Words

chill	sniff	brass
jazz	muff	sell
bell	kiss	glass
mess		

〔Offline〕 ⏱ 15 minutes per day

Complete the Spelling activities with students. **For the full instructions for each activity, refer to pages SP 8–13.**

Day 1

Introduce Heart Words and Double Trouble Endings

〔Materials〕

- index cards (25)
- whiteboard (optional)

Advance Preparation

Write each Heart, Target, Challenge, and Alternate Word on a separate index card. Indicate on each card whether a word is a Heart, Target, Challenge, or Alternate Word.

Pretest

1. **Administer** a pretest using the Heart and Target Words.

2. **Gather** students' Words to Learn cards.

Note: If students didn't misspell any Heart, Target, Challenge, or Alternate Words, mark lessons 2 and 3 complete and move to the online activity for Day 4 to practice for the Unit Checkpoint on Day 5.

Heart Words

➲ *Skip this activity if students didn't misspell any Heart Words on this unit's pretest.*

1. **Gather** the Words to Learn cards for any Heart Words.

2. **Practice** the *new* Heart Words.

3. **Practice** *all* Heart Words.

4. **Track mastery** of Heart Words.

Target Words

➲ *Skip this activity if students didn't misspell any Target Words on this unit's pretest.*

1. **Gather** the Words to Learn cards for any Target Words.

2. **Discover** the new spelling convention.

3. **Practice** the Target Words.

Challenge Words

➲ *Skip this activity if students are struggling with the Heart Words and Target Words.*

1. **Gather** the Words to Learn cards for any Challenge Words.
2. **Discover** the new spelling convention in the Challenge Words.
3. **Practice** the Challenge Words.

Alternate Words

➲ *Skip this activity if students don't have any Words to Learn cards for Alternate Words.*

1. **Gather** the Words to Learn cards for any Alternate Words.
2. **Discover** the new spelling convention in the Alternate Words.
3. **Practice** the Alternate Words.

Day 2 ···

Practice Spelling Words

Practice using the Activity Bank.

Day 3 ···

Practice Spelling Words

Practice using the Activity Bank.

 **15 minutes**

Day 4 ···

Review Spelling Words

Review using the online activity.

[Offline] ⑮ minutes

Unit Checkpoint

1. **Dictate** the Heart Words and Target Words.

2. **Check** students' answers.

3. **Review** the words students misspelled.

Rewards:

- If students scored 80 percent or above on the Unit Checkpoint, add a sticker to the Unit 7 box on students' My Accomplishments chart. If students scored under 80 percent, continue to practice the words that they missed and add a sticker to this unit once they have mastered the words.

- Help students find and play the online Spelling game, Spell 'n' Stack. Students should use level 1.

Heart Words and *r*-Controlled Vowels

Target spelling convention – the sounds of short vowels when followed by the letter *r*

The sound of a short vowel changes when it is followed by *r*. The letter combinations *er*, *ir*, and *ur* all sound like /er/. The letter combination *ar* sounds like /ar/. The letter combination *or* sounds like /or/. Each of this unit's Target Words contains an *r*-controlled vowel.

Objectives
- Spell Heart Words.
- Spell words containing the *r*-controlled vowels *ar, ir, er, or,* or *ur*.

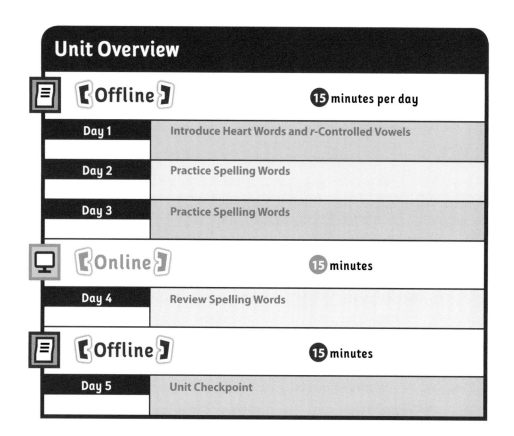

Unit Overview

Offline — 15 minutes per day

Day 1	Introduce Heart Words and *r*-Controlled Vowels
Day 2	Practice Spelling Words
Day 3	Practice Spelling Words

Online — 15 minutes

| Day 4 | Review Spelling Words |

Offline — 15 minutes

| Day 5 | Unit Checkpoint |

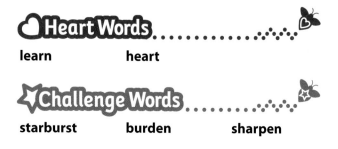

Heart Words

learn   heart

Challenge Words

starburst   burden   sharpen

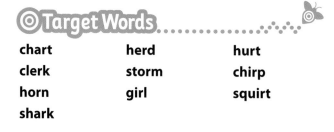

Target Words

chart	herd	hurt
clerk	storm	chirp
horn	girl	squirt
shark		

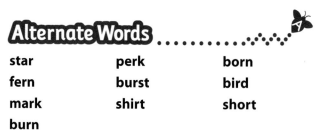

Alternate Words

star	perk	born
fern	burst	bird
mark	shirt	short
burn		

# [Offline] ⏱ minutes per day

Complete the Spelling activities with students. **For the full instructions for each activity, refer to pages SP 8–13.**

 Day 1 ···

Introduce Heart Words and *r*-Controlled Vowels

[Materials]

- index cards (25)
- whiteboard (optional)

Advance Preparation

Write each Heart, Target, Challenge, and Alternate Word on a separate index card. Indicate on each card whether a word is a Heart, Target, Challenge, or Alternate Word.

Pretest

1. **Administer** a pretest using the Heart and Target Words.

2. **Gather** students' Words to Learn cards.

Note: If students didn't misspell any Heart, Target, Challenge, or Alternate Words, mark lessons 2 and 3 complete and move to the online activity for Day 4 to practice for the Unit Checkpoint on Day 5.

Heart Words

➲ *Skip this activity if students didn't misspell any Heart Words on this unit's pretest.*

1. **Gather** the Words to Learn cards for any Heart Words.

2. **Practice** the *new* Heart Words.

3. **Practice** *all* Heart Words.

4. **Track mastery** of Heart Words.

Target Words

➲ *Skip this activity if students didn't misspell any Target Words on this unit's pretest.*

1. **Gather** the Words to Learn cards for any Target Words.

2. **Discover** the new spelling convention.

3. **Practice** the Target Words.

Challenge Words

⮑ *Skip this activity if students are struggling with the Heart Words and Target Words.*

1. **Gather** the Words to Learn cards for any Challenge Words.
2. **Discover** the new spelling convention in the Challenge Words.
3. **Practice** the Challenge Words.

Alternate Words

⮑ *Skip this activity if students don't have any Words to Learn cards for Alternate Words.*

1. **Gather** the Words to Learn cards for any Alternate Words.
2. **Discover** the new spelling convention in the Alternate Words.
3. **Practice** the Alternate Words.

Day 2

Practice Spelling Words

Practice using the Activity Bank.

Day 3

Practice Spelling Words

Practice using the Activity Bank.

 **15 minutes**

Day 4

Review Spelling Words

Review using the online activity.

Day 5

Unit Checkpoint

1. **Dictate** the Heart Words and Target Words.

2. **Check** students' answers.

3. **Review** the words students misspelled.

Rewards:

- If students scored 80 percent or above on the Unit Checkpoint, add a sticker to the Unit 8 box on students' My Accomplishments chart. If students scored under 80 percent, continue to practice the words that they missed and add a sticker to this unit once they have mastered the words.

- Help students find and play the online Spelling game, Spell 'n' Stack. Students should use level 1.

Heart Words and Long *a* Spellings

Target spelling convention – **letter combinations that create the long *a* sound**

We can spell the long *a* sound with the letters *ai*, *ay*, *ea*, or the letter *a*, followed by a consonant and then a silent *e*. Each of this unit's Target Words contains the long *a* sound spelled with one of these letter combinations.

Objectives
- Spell Heart Words.
- Spell words containing the long *a* sound spelled *ai*, *ay*, *ea*, or *a*-consonant-*e*.

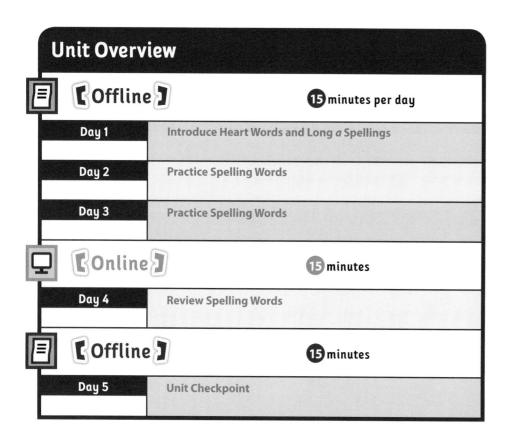

Unit Overview

📄 〖Offline〗 ⏱15 minutes per day

Day 1	Introduce Heart Words and Long *a* Spellings
Day 2	Practice Spelling Words
Day 3	Practice Spelling Words

🖥 〖Online〗 ⏱15 minutes

| Day 4 | Review Spelling Words |

📄 〖Offline〗 ⏱15 minutes

| Day 5 | Unit Checkpoint |

☁ Heart Words

have	shall

⭐ Challenge Words

painful	playmate	railway

◎ Target Words

flame	great	play
rain	plate	steak
gray	paint	sprain
mail		

Alternate Words

shame	pay	break
slate	say	skate
pain	sail	strain
quaint		

 **Offline** **15** minutes per day

Complete the Spelling activities with students. **For the full instructions for each activity, refer to pages SP 8–13.**

Day 1

Introduce Heart Words and Long *a* Spellings

Materials

- index cards (25)
- whiteboard (optional)

Advance Preparation

Write each Heart, Target, Challenge, and Alternate Word on a separate index card. Indicate on each card whether a word is a Heart, Target, Challenge, or Alternate Word.

Pretest

1. **Administer** a pretest using the Heart and Target Words.

2. **Gather** students' Words to Learn cards.

Note: If students didn't misspell any Heart, Target, Challenge, or Alternate Words, mark lessons 2 and 3 complete and move to the online activity for Day 4 to practice for the Unit Checkpoint on Day 5.

Heart Words

➲ *Skip this activity if students didn't misspell any Heart Words on this unit's pretest.*

1. **Gather** the Words to Learn cards for any Heart Words.

2. **Practice** the *new* Heart Words.

3. **Practice** *all* Heart Words.

4. **Track mastery** of Heart Words.

Target Words

➲ *Skip this activity if students didn't misspell any Target Words on this unit's pretest.*

1. **Gather** the Words to Learn cards for any Target Words.

2. **Discover** the new spelling convention.

3. **Practice** the Target Words.

Challenge Words

➲ *Skip this activity if students are struggling with the Heart Words and Target Words.*

1. **Gather** the Words to Learn cards for any Challenge Words.
2. **Discover** the new spelling convention in the Challenge Words.
3. **Practice** the Challenge Words.

Alternate Words

➲ *Skip this activity if students don't have any Words to Learn cards for Alternate Words.*

1. **Gather** the Words to Learn cards for any Alternate Words.
2. **Discover** the new spelling convention in the Alternate Words.
3. **Practice** the Alternate Words.

Day 2 ···

Practice Spelling Words

Practice using the Activity Bank.

Day 3 ···

Practice Spelling Words

Practice using the Activity Bank.

 **15 minutes**

Day 4 ···

Review Spelling Words

Review using the online activity.

[Offline] 🕐 minutes

Day 5

Unit Checkpoint

1. **Dictate** the Heart Words and Target Words.

2. **Check** students' answers.

3. **Review** the words students misspelled.

Rewards:

- If students scored 80 percent or above on the Unit Checkpoint, add a sticker to the Unit 9 box on students' My Accomplishments chart. If students scored under 80 percent, continue to practice the words that they missed and add a sticker to this unit once they have mastered the words.

- Help students find and play the online Spelling game, Spell 'n' Stack. Students should use level 1.

Heart Words and Long *i* Spellings

Target spelling convention – **letter combinations that create the long *i* sound**

We can spell the long *i* sound with the letters *ie*, *igh*, the letter *i* followed by a consonant and then a silent *e*, or even the letter *i* by itself. Each of this unit's Target Words contains the long *i* sound spelled with one of these letter combinations.

Objectives
- Spell Heart Words.
- Spell words containing the long *i* sound spelled *ie*, *igh*, *i*, or *i*-consonant-*e*.

Unit Overview

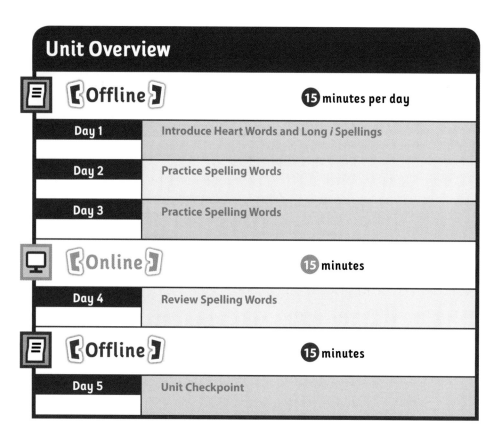

Offline — 15 minutes per day

Day 1	Introduce Heart Words and Long *i* Spellings
Day 2	Practice Spelling Words
Day 3	Practice Spelling Words

Online — 15 minutes

| Day 4 | Review Spelling Words |

Offline — 15 minutes

| Day 5 | Unit Checkpoint |

Heart Words

write	straight

Challenge Words

parasite	hindsight	necktie

Target Words

slide	fright	bright
high	mind	time
stripe	wild	sunlight
pie		

Alternate Words

wide	wipe	chime
kind	sight	might
sigh	tie	wind
child		

 **15** minutes per day

Complete the Spelling activities with students. **For the full instructions for each activity, refer to pages SP 8–13.**

 ....

Introduce Heart Words and Long *i* Spellings

[Materials]

- index cards (25)
- whiteboard (optional)

Advance Preparation

Write each Heart, Target, Challenge, and Alternate Word on a separate index card. Indicate on each card whether a word is a Heart, Target, Challenge, or Alternate Word.

Pretest

1. **Administer** a pretest using the Heart and Target Words.

2. **Gather** students' Words to Learn cards.

Note: If students didn't misspell any Heart, Target, Challenge, or Alternate Words, mark Lessons 2 and 3 complete and move to the online activity for Day 4 to practice for the Unit Checkpoint on Day 5.

Heart Words

➲ *Skip this activity if students didn't misspell any Heart Words on this unit's pretest.*

1. **Gather** the Words to Learn cards for any Heart Words.

2. **Practice** the *new* Heart Words.

3. **Practice** *all* Heart Words.

4. **Track mastery** of Heart Words.

Target Words

➲ *Skip this activity if students didn't misspell any Target Words on this unit's pretest.*

1. **Gather** the Words to Learn cards for any Target Words.

2. **Discover** the new spelling convention.

3. **Practice** the Target Words.

Challenge Words

⮑ *Skip this activity if students are struggling with the Heart Words and Target Words.*

1. **Gather** the Words to Learn cards for any Challenge Words.

2. **Discover** the new spelling convention in the Challenge Words.

3. **Practice** the Challenge Words.

Alternate Words

⮑ *Skip this activity if students don't have any Words to Learn cards for Alternate Words.*

1. **Gather** the Words to Learn cards for any Alternate Words.

2. **Discover** the new spelling convention in the Alternate Words.

3. **Practice** the Alternate Words.

Day 2 ....

Practice Spelling Words

Practice using the Activity Bank.

Day 3 ....

Practice Spelling Words

Practice using the Activity Bank.

 **15 minutes**

Day 4 ....

Review Spelling Words

Review using the online activity.

[Offline] **15** minutes

Day 5

Unit Checkpoint

1. **Dictate** the Heart Words and Target Words.

2. **Check** students' answers.

3. **Review** the words students misspelled.

Rewards:

- If students scored 80 percent or above on the Unit Checkpoint, add a sticker to the Unit 10 box on students' My Accomplishments chart. If students scored under 80 percent, continue to practice the words that they missed and add a sticker to this unit once they have mastered the words.

- Help students find and play the online Spelling game, Spell 'n' Stack. Students should use level 1.

Heart Words and Long *o* Spellings

Target spelling convention — **letter combinations that create the long *o* sound**

We can spell the long *o* sound with the letters *oa*, *oe*, the letter *o* followed by a consonant and then a silent *e*, or even the letter *o* by itself. Each of this unit's Target Words contains the long *o* sound spelled with one of these letter combinations.

Objectives
- Spell Heart Words.
- Spell words containing the long *o* sound spelled *oa*, *oe*, *o*, or *o-consonant-e*.

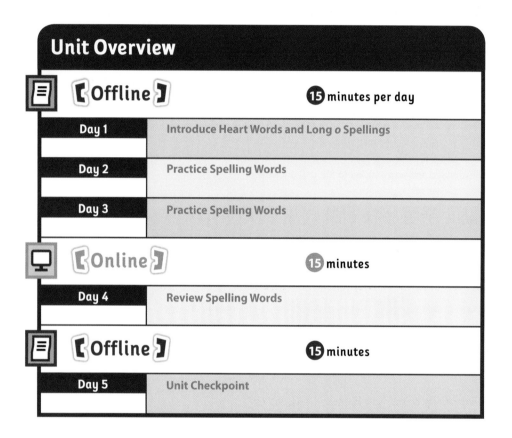

Unit Overview

📋 〖Offline〗 ⑮ **minutes per day**

Day 1	Introduce Heart Words and Long *o* Spellings
Day 2	Practice Spelling Words
Day 3	Practice Spelling Words

💻 〖Online〗 ⑮ **minutes**

Day 4	Review Spelling Words

📋 〖Offline〗 ⑮ **minutes**

Day 5	Unit Checkpoint

♡ Heart Words

none	some	come

✭ Challenge Words

snowflake	rainbow	overbite

◎ Target Words

most	broke	boast
throat	toe	colt
blown	snow	slope
scold		

Alternate Words

post	flown	jolt
hoe	toast	smoke
float	cold	hope
glow		

[Offline] ⑮ minutes per day

Complete the Spelling activities with students. **For the full instructions for each activity, refer to pages SP 8–13.**

Day 1 ....

Introduce Heart Words and Long *o* Spellings

[Materials]

- index cards (26)
- whiteboard (optional)

Advance Preparation

Write each Heart, Target, Challenge, and Alternate Word on a separate index card. Indicate on each card whether a word is a Heart, Target, Challenge, or Alternate Word.

Pretest

1. **Administer** a pretest using the Heart and Target Words.

2. **Gather** students' Words to Learn cards.

Note: If students didn't misspell any Heart, Target, Challenge, or Alternate Words, mark Lessons 2 and 3 complete and move to the online activity for Day 4 to practice for the Unit Checkpoint on Day 5.

Heart Words

⊃ *Skip this activity if students didn't misspell any Heart Words on this unit's pretest.*

1. **Gather** the Words to Learn cards for any Heart Words.

2. **Practice** the *new* Heart Words.

3. **Practice** *all* Heart Words.

4. **Track mastery** of Heart Words.

Target Words

⊃ *Skip this activity if students didn't misspell any Target Words on this unit's pretest.*

1. **Gather** the Words to Learn cards for any Target Words.

2. **Discover** the new spelling convention.

3. **Practice** the Target Words.

Challenge Words

⮑ *Skip this activity if students are struggling with the Heart Words and Target Words.*

1. **Gather** the Words to Learn cards for any Challenge Words.
2. **Discover** the new spelling convention in the Challenge Words.
3. **Practice** the Challenge Words.

Alternate Words

⮑ *Skip this activity if students don't have any Words to Learn cards for Alternate Words.*

1. **Gather** the Words to Learn cards for any Alternate Words.
2. **Discover** the new spelling convention in the Alternate Words.
3. **Practice** the Alternate Words.

Day 2 ....

Practice Spelling Words
Practice using the Activity Bank.

Day 3 ....

Practice Spelling Words
Practice using the Activity Bank.

 minutes

Day 4 ....

Review Spelling Words
Review using the online activity.

 **Offline** ⏱ **15 minutes**

Day 5

Unit Checkpoint

1. **Dictate** the Heart Words and Target Words.

2. **Check** students' answers.

3. **Review** the words students misspelled.

 Rewards:

- If students scored 80 percent or above on the Unit Checkpoint, add a sticker to the Unit 11 box on students' My Accomplishments chart. If students scored under 80 percent, continue to practice the words that they missed and add a sticker to this unit once they have mastered the words.

- Help students find and play the online Spelling game, Spell 'n' Stack. Students should use level 1.

Review Heart Words, Double Endings, *r*-Controlled Vowels, and Long Vowel Spellings

In this unit, students will review the spelling conventions and Heart Words they studied in the previous five units. Refer back to the Unit Plans of previous units for a detailed description of each spelling convention.

Objectives

- Spell Heart Words.
- Spell words ending with the double letters *ss, zz, ll,* or *ff*.
- Spell words containing the *r*-controlled vowels *ar, ir, er, or,* or *ur*.
- Spell words containing the long *a* sound spelled *ai, ay, ea,* or *a-consonant-e*.
- Spell words containing the long *i* sound spelled *ie, igh, i,* or *i-consonant-e*.
- Spell words containing the long *o* sound spelled *oa, oe, o,* or *o-consonant-e*.

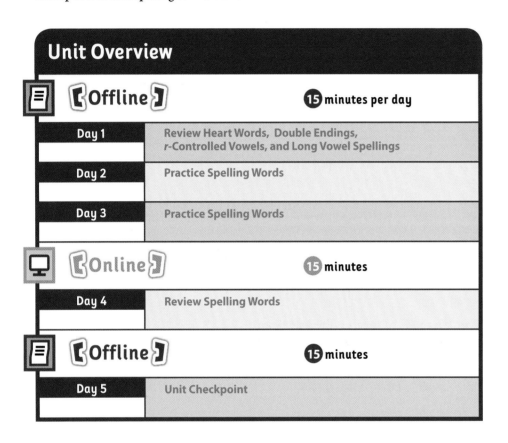

Unit Overview

[Offline]   15 minutes per day

Day 1	Review Heart Words, Double Endings, *r*-Controlled Vowels, and Long Vowel Spellings
Day 2	Practice Spelling Words
Day 3	Practice Spelling Words

[Online]   15 minutes

Day 4	Review Spelling Words

[Offline]   15 minutes

Day 5	Unit Checkpoint

Heart Words

half	have	none
truth	shall	some
learn	write	come
heart	straight	

Challenge Words

playwright	airline	baseboard

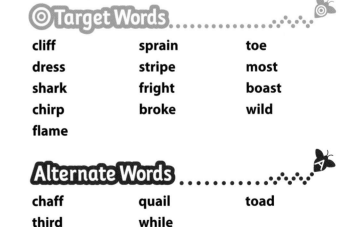

Target Words

cliff	sprain	toe
dress	stripe	most
shark	fright	boast
chirp	broke	wild
flame		

Alternate Words

chaff	quail	toad
third	while	

[Offline] ⏰ 15 minutes per day

Complete the Spelling activities with students. **For the full instructions for each activity, refer to pages SP 8–13.**

Day 1

Review Heart Words, Double Endings, *r*-Controlled Vowels, and Long Vowel Spellings

[Materials]

- index cards (8)
- whiteboard (optional)

Advance Preparation

Gather the index cards you made previously for the Heart and Target Words listed. Write each Challenge and Alternate Word on a separate index card. Indicate on each card whether a word is a Challenge or Alternate Word.

Pretest

1. **Administer** a pretest using the Heart and Target Words.

2. **Gather** students' Words to Learn cards.

Note: If students didn't misspell any Heart, Target, Challenge, or Alternate Words, mark Lessons 2 and 3 complete and move to the online activity for Day 4 to practice for the Unit Checkpoint on Day 5.

Heart Words

➲ *Skip this activity if students didn't misspell any Heart Words on this unit's pretest.*

1. **Gather** the Words to Learn cards for any Heart Words.

2. **Practice** the Heart Words.

3. **Track mastery** of Heart Words.

Target Words

➲ *Skip this activity if students didn't misspell any Target Words on this unit's pretest.*

1. **Gather** the Words to Learn cards for any Target Words.

2. **Review** the previously studied spelling convention in each Target Word.

3. **Practice** the Target Words.

Challenge Words

➲ *Skip this activity if students are struggling with the Heart Words and Target Words.*

1. **Gather** the Words to Learn cards for any Challenge Words.
2. **Review** the previously studied spelling convention in each Challenge Word.
3. **Practice** the Challenge Words.

Alternate Words

➲ *Skip this activity if students don't have any Words to Learn cards for Alternate Words.*

1. **Gather** the Words to Learn cards for any Alternate Words.
2. **Review** the previously studied spelling convention in each Alternate Word.
3. **Practice** the Alternate Words.

Day 2 ....

Practice Spelling Words

Practice using the Activity Bank.

Day 3 ....

Practice Spelling Words

Practice using the Activity Bank.

 **15 minutes**

Day 4 ....

Review Spelling Words

Review using the online activity.

[Offline] 🕒 minutes

Unit Checkpoint

1. **Dictate** the Heart Words and Target Words.

2. **Check** students' answers.

3. **Review** the words students misspelled.

Rewards:

- If students scored 80 percent or above on the Unit Checkpoint, add a sticker to the Unit 12 box on students' My Accomplishments chart. If students scored under 80 percent, continue to practice the words that they missed and add a sticker to this unit once they have mastered the words.

- Help students find and play the online Spelling game, Spell 'n' Stack. Students should use level 1.

Heart Words and Long *e* Spellings (A)

Target spelling convention — **letter combinations that create the long *e* sound**

We can spell the long *e* sound with the letters *ee, ea*, the letter *e* followed by a consonant and then a silent *e*, or even the letter *e* by itself. Each of this unit's Target Words contains the long *e* sound spelled with one of these letter combinations.

Objectives
- Spell Heart Words.
- Spell words containing the long *e* sound spelled *ee, ea, e,* or *e-consonant-e*.

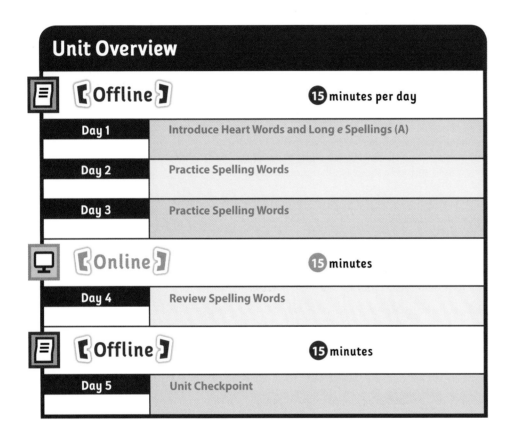

Unit Overview		
Offline		**15** minutes per day
Day 1	Introduce Heart Words and Long *e* Spellings (A)	
Day 2	Practice Spelling Words	
Day 3	Practice Spelling Words	
Online		**15** minutes
Day 4	Review Spelling Words	
Offline		**15** minutes
Day 5	Unit Checkpoint	

Heart Words

eye	been	where

Challenge Words

weekend	screeched	repeat

Target Words

dream	cheeks	sweep
three	speak	treat
need	street	team
these		

Alternate Words

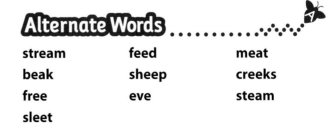

stream	feed	meat
beak	sheep	creeks
free	eve	steam
sleet		

[Offline] 🕐 minutes per day

Complete the Spelling activities with students. **For the full instructions for each activity, refer to pages SP 8–13.**

Day 1 ....

Introduce Heart Words and Long *e* Spellings (A)

[Materials]

- index cards (26)
- whiteboard (optional)

Advance Preparation

Write each Heart, Target, Challenge, and Alternate Word on a separate index card. Indicate on each card whether a word is a Heart, Target, Challenge, or Alternate Word.

Pretest

1. **Administer** a pretest using the Heart and Target Words.

2. **Gather** students' Words to Learn cards.

Note: If students didn't misspell any Heart, Target, Challenge, or Alternate Words, mark Lessons 2 and 3 complete and move to the online activity for Day 4 to practice for the Unit Checkpoint on Day 5.

Heart Words

⮌ *Skip this activity if students didn't misspell any Heart Words on this unit's pretest.*

1. **Gather** the Words to Learn cards for any Heart Words.

2. **Practice** the *new* Heart Words.

3. **Practice** *all* Heart Words.

4. **Track mastery** of Heart Words.

Target Words

⮌ *Skip this activity if students didn't misspell any Target Words on this unit's pretest.*

1. **Gather** the Words to Learn cards for any Target Words.

2. **Discover** the new spelling convention.

3. **Practice** the Target Words.

Challenge Words

⮑ *Skip this activity if students are struggling with the Heart Words and Target Words.*

1. **Gather** the Words to Learn cards for any Challenge Words.
2. **Discover** the new spelling convention in the Challenge Words.
3. **Practice** the Challenge Words.

Alternate Words

⮑ *Skip this activity if students don't have any Words to Learn cards for Alternate Words.*

1. **Gather** the Words to Learn cards for any Alternate Words.
2. **Discover** the new spelling convention in the Alternate Words.
3. **Practice** the Alternate Words.

Day 2 ....

Practice Spelling Words

Practice using the Activity Bank.

Day 3 ....

Practice Spelling Words

Practice using the Activity Bank.

 **minutes**

Day 4 ....

Review Spelling Words

Review using the online activity.

 **15** minutes

Day 5

Unit Checkpoint

1. **Dictate** the Heart Words and Target Words.

2. **Check** students' answers.

3. **Review** the words students misspelled.

 Rewards:

- If students scored 80 percent or above on the Unit Checkpoint, add a sticker to the Unit 13 box on students' My Accomplishments chart. If students scored under 80 percent, continue to practice the words that they missed and add a sticker to this unit once they have mastered the words.

- Help students find and play the online Spelling game, Spell 'n' Stack. Students should use level 1.

Heart Words and Long *e* Spellings (B)

Target spelling convention – **letter combinations that create the long *e* sound**

We can spell the long *e* sound with the letters *ey* or *ie*. Each of this unit's Target Words contains the long *e* sound spelled with one of these letter combinations.

Objectives
- Spell Heart Words.
- Spell words containing the long *e* sound spelled *ey* or *ie*.

Unit Overview

▤ 〔Offline〕 **15** minutes per day

Day 1	Introduce Heart Words and Long *e* Spellings(B)
Day 2	Practice Spelling Words
Day 3	Practice Spelling Words

🖥 〔Online〕 **15** minutes

| Day 4 | Review Spelling Words |

▤ 〔Offline〕 **15** minutes

| Day 5 | Unit Checkpoint |

♡ Heart Words

| they | guess | guest |

☆ Challenge Words

| belief | believe | monkey |

◎ Target Words

yield	key	grieve
field	hockey	priest
shield	chief	brief
pier		

Alternate Words

shriek	wield	piece
jockey	relief	turkey
fields	tier	thief
grief		

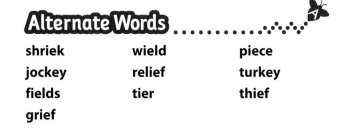

[Offline] ⏱ 15 minutes per day

Complete the Spelling activities with students. **For the full instructions for each activity, refer to pages SP 8–13.**

Day 1 ....

Introduce Heart Words and Long *e* Spellings (B)

[Materials]

• index cards (26)
• whiteboard (optional)

Advance Preparation

Write each Heart, Target, Challenge, and Alternate Word on a separate index card. Indicate on each card whether a word is a Heart, Target, Challenge, or Alternate Word.

Pretest

1. **Administer** a pretest using the Heart and Target Words.

2. **Gather** students' Words to Learn cards.

Note: If students didn't misspell any Heart, Target, Challenge, or Alternate Words, mark Lessons 2 and 3 complete and move to the online activity for Day 4 to practice for the Unit Checkpoint on Day 5.

Heart Words

➲ *Skip this activity if students didn't misspell any Heart Words on this unit's pretest.*

1. **Gather** the Words to Learn cards for any Heart Words.

2. **Practice** the *new* Heart Words.

3. **Practice** *all* Heart Words.

4. **Track mastery** of Heart Words.

Target Words

➲ *Skip this activity if students didn't misspell any Target Words on this unit's pretest.*

1. **Gather** the Words to Learn cards for any Target Words.

2. **Discover** the new spelling convention.

3. **Practice** the Target Words.

Challenge Words

➲ *Skip this activity if students are struggling with the Heart Words and Target Words.*

1. **Gather** the Words to Learn cards for any Challenge Words.
2. **Discover** the new spelling convention in the Challenge Words.
3. **Practice** the Challenge Words.

Alternate Words

➲ *Skip this activity if students don't have any Words to Learn cards for Alternate Words.*

1. **Gather** the Words to Learn cards for any Alternate Words.
2. **Discover** the new spelling convention in the Alternate Words.
3. **Practice** the Alternate Words.

Day 2 ....

Practice Spelling Words

Practice using the Activity Bank.

Day 3 ....

Practice Spelling Words

Practice using the Activity Bank.

 **15 minutes**

Day 4 ....

Review Spelling Words

Review using the online activity.

[Offline] ⏱ **15** minutes

Unit Checkpoint

1. **Dictate** the Heart Words and Target Words.

2. **Check** students' answers.

3. **Review** the words students misspelled.

Rewards:

- If students scored 80 percent or above on the Unit Checkpoint, add a sticker to the Unit 14 box on students' My Accomplishments chart. If students scored under 80 percent, continue to practice the words that they missed and add a sticker to this unit once they have mastered the words.

- Help students find and play the online Spelling game, Spell 'n' Stack. Students should use level 1.

Heart Words and Long *u* Spellings

Target spelling convention — **letter combinations that create the long *u* sound**

We can spell the long *u* sound with the letters *ue*, *ew*, the letter *u* followed by a consonant and then a silent *e*, or even the letter *u* by itself. Each of this unit's Target Words contains the long *u* sound spelled with one of these letter combinations.

Objectives
- Spell Heart Words.
- Spell words containing the long *u* sound spelled *ue*, *ew*, *u*, or *u-consonant-e*.

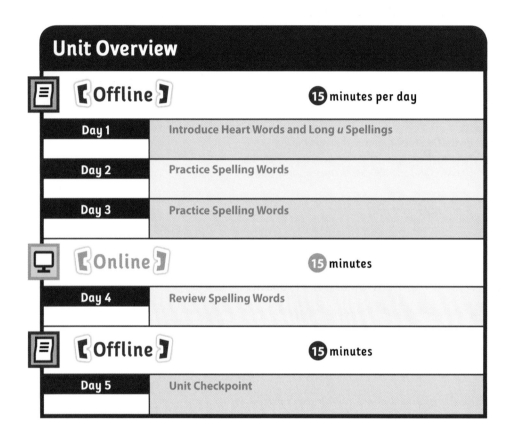

Unit Overview

📋 〔Offline〕 **15** minutes per day

Day 1	Introduce Heart Words and Long *u* Spellings
Day 2	Practice Spelling Words
Day 3	Practice Spelling Words

🖥 〔Online〕 **15** minutes

| Day 4 | Review Spelling Words |

📋 〔Offline〕 **15** minutes

| Day 5 | Unit Checkpoint |

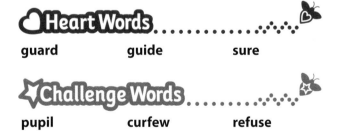

Heart Words

| guard | guide | sure |

Challenge Words

| pupil | curfew | refuse |

Target Words

cute	rescue	few
use	unite	cube
unit	hue	cue
mule		

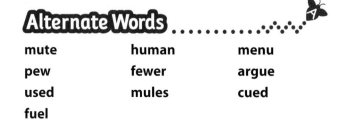

Alternate Words

mute	human	menu
pew	fewer	argue
used	mules	cued
fuel		

 **15 minutes per day**

Complete the Spelling activities with students. **For the full instructions for each activity, refer to pages SP 8–13.**

Day 1

Introduce Heart Words and Long *u* Spellings

Materials

- index cards (26)
- whiteboard (optional)

Advance Preparation

Write each Heart, Target, Challenge, and Alternate Word on a separate index card. Indicate on each card whether a word is a Heart, Target, Challenge, or Alternate Word.

Pretest

1. **Administer** a pretest using the Heart and Target Words.

2. **Gather** students' Words to Learn cards.

Note: If students didn't misspell any Heart, Target, Challenge, or Alternate Words, mark Lessons 2 and 3 complete and move to the online activity for Day 4 to practice for the Unit Checkpoint on Day 5.

Heart Words

➲ *Skip this activity if students didn't misspell any Heart Words on this unit's pretest.*

1. **Gather** the Words to Learn cards for any Heart Words.

2. **Practice** the *new* Heart Words.

3. **Practice** *all* Heart Words.

4. **Track mastery** of Heart Words.

Target Words

➲ *Skip this activity if students didn't misspell any Target Words on this unit's pretest.*

1. **Gather** the Words to Learn cards for any Target Words.

2. **Discover** the new spelling convention.

3. **Practice** the Target Words.

Challenge Words

➲ *Skip this activity if students are struggling with the Heart Words and Target Words.*

1. **Gather** the Words to Learn cards for any Challenge Words.

2. **Discover** the new spelling convention in the Challenge Words.

3. **Practice** the Challenge Words.

Alternate Words

➲ *Skip this activity if students don't have any Words to Learn cards for Alternate Words.*

1. **Gather** the Words to Learn cards for any Alternate Words.

2. **Discover** the new spelling convention in the Alternate Words.

3. **Practice** the Alternate Words.

Day 2 ....

Practice Spelling Words

Practice using the Activity Bank.

Day 3 ....

Practice Spelling Words

Practice using the Activity Bank.

 **15 minutes**

Day 4 ....

Review Spelling Words

Review using the online activity.

 **15** minutes

Unit Checkpoint

1. **Dictate** the Heart Words and Target Words.

2. **Check** students' answers.

3. **Review** the words students misspelled.

 Rewards:

- If students scored 80 percent or above on the Unit Checkpoint, add a sticker to the Unit 15 box on students' My Accomplishments chart. If students scored under 80 percent, continue to practice the words that they missed and add a sticker to this unit once they have mastered the words.

- Help students find and play the online Spelling game, Spell 'n' Stack. Students should use level 1.

Heart Words and Long Double *o* Spellings

Target spelling convention – **letter combinations that create the long double *o* sound**

We can spell the long double *o* sound, as in the words *glue* and *spool*, with the letters *ue*, *ew*, *oo*, or the letter *u* followed by a consonant and then a silent *e*. Each of this unit's Target Words contains the long double *o* sound spelled with one of these letter combinations.

Objectives
- Spell Heart Words.
- Spell words containing the long double *o* sound spelled *ue*, *ew*, *oo*, or *u*-consonant-*e*.

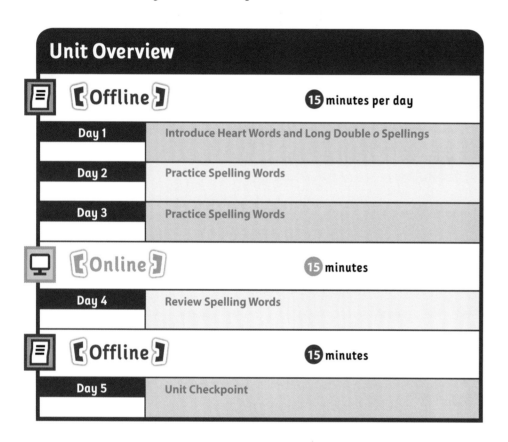

Unit Overview

📋 ❰Offline❱   **⑮ minutes per day**

Day 1	Introduce Heart Words and Long Double *o* Spellings
Day 2	Practice Spelling Words
Day 3	Practice Spelling Words

💻 ❰Online❱   **⑮ minutes**

| Day 4 | Review Spelling Words |

📋 ❰Offline❱   **⑮ minutes**

| Day 5 | Unit Checkpoint |

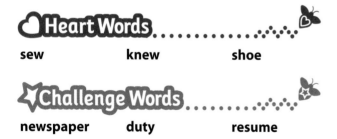

☁ Heart Words ....

sew	knew	shoe

⭐ Challenge Words ....

newspaper	duty	resume

◎ Target Words ....

June	tooth	screw
glue	clue	untrue
spool	tube	threw
food		

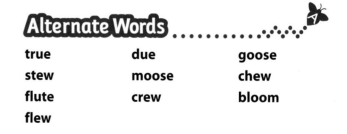

Alternate Words ....

true	due	goose
stew	moose	chew
flute	crew	bloom
flew		

[Offline] ⏱ 15 minutes per day

Complete the Spelling activities with students. **For the full instructions for each activity, refer to pages SP 8–13.**

Day 1 ●

Introduce Heart Words and Long Double *o* Spellings

[Materials]

- index cards (26)
- whiteboard (optional)

Advance Preparation

Write each Heart, Target, Challenge, and Alternate Word on a separate index card. Indicate on each card whether a word is a Heart, Target, Challenge, or Alternate Word.

Pretest

1. **Administer** a pretest using the Heart and Target Words.

2. **Gather** students' Words to Learn cards.

Note: If students didn't misspell any Heart, Target, Challenge, or Alternate Words, mark Lessons 2 and 3 complete and move to the online activity for Day 4 to practice for the Unit Checkpoint on Day 5.

Heart Words

➲ *Skip this activity if students didn't misspell any Heart Words on this unit's pretest.*

1. **Gather** the Words to Learn cards for any Heart Words.

2. **Practice** the *new* Heart Words.

3. **Practice** *all* Heart Words.

4. **Track mastery** of Heart Words.

Target Words

➲ *Skip this activity if students didn't misspell any Target Words on this unit's pretest.*

1. **Gather** the Words to Learn cards for any Target Words.

2. **Discover** the new spelling convention.

3. **Practice** the Target Words.

Challenge Words

⮕ *Skip this activity if students are struggling with the Heart Words and Target Words.*

1. **Gather** the Words to Learn cards for any Challenge Words.
2. **Discover** the new spelling convention in the Challenge Words.
3. **Practice** the Challenge Words.

Alternate Words

⮕ *Skip this activity if students don't have any Words to Learn cards for Alternate Words.*

1. **Gather** the Words to Learn cards for any Alternate Words.
2. **Discover** the new spelling convention in the Alternate Words.
3. **Practice** the Alternate Words.

Day 2 ···

Practice Spelling Words

Practice using the Activity Bank.

Day 3 ···

Practice Spelling Words

Practice using the Activity Bank.

 **15 minutes**

Day 4 ···

Review Spelling Words

Review using the online activity.

[Offline] ⑮ minutes

Unit Checkpoint

1. **Dictate** the Heart Words and Target Words.

2. **Check** students' answers.

3. **Review** the words students misspelled.

Rewards:

- If students scored 80 percent or above on the Unit Checkpoint, add a sticker to the Unit 16 box on students' My Accomplishments chart. If students scored under 80 percent, continue to practice the words that they missed and add a sticker to this unit once they have mastered the words.

- Help students find and play the online Spelling game, Spell 'n' Stack. Students should use level 1.

Heart Words and Short Double *o* & /ow/ Spellings

Target spelling convention — **creating the short double *o* sound with the letters *oo*; letter combinations that create the sound /ow/**

We can spell the short double *o* sound with the letters *oo*. We can spell the sound /ow/ with the letters *ou* or *ow*. This unit's Target Words contain one of these sounds.

Objectives

- Spell Heart Words.
- Spell words containing the short double *o* sound spelled *oo*.
- Spell words containing the sound /ow/ spelled *ou* or *ow*.

Unit Overview

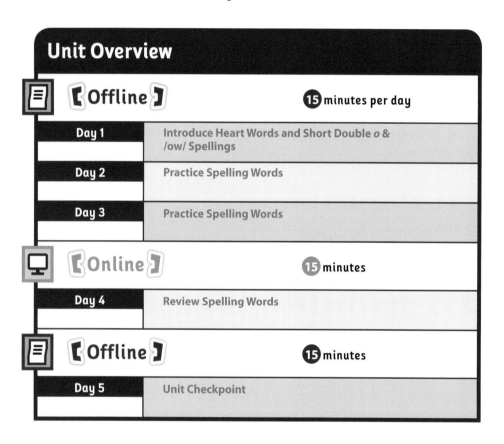

📋 〖Offline〗 🕒 **15 minutes per day**

Day 1	Introduce Heart Words and Short Double *o* & /ow/ Spellings
Day 2	Practice Spelling Words
Day 3	Practice Spelling Words

🖥 〖Online〗 🕒 **15 minutes**

| Day 4 | Review Spelling Words |

📋 〖Offline〗 🕒 **15 minutes**

| Day 5 | Unit Checkpoint |

❤ Heart Words

| could | would | should |

⭐ Challenge Words

| flower | downtown | overlook |

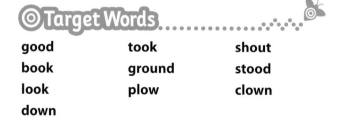

◎ Target Words

good	took	shout
book	ground	stood
look	plow	clown
down		

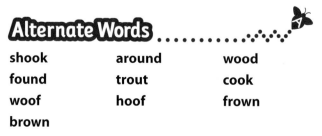

Alternate Words

shook	around	wood
found	trout	cook
woof	hoof	frown
brown		

 **15** minutes per day

Complete the Spelling activities with students. **For the full instructions for each activity, refer to pages SP 8–13.**

Day 1 ....

Introduce Heart Words and Short Double *o* & /ow/ Spellings

- index cards (26)
- whiteboard (optional)

Advance Preparation

Write each Heart, Target, Challenge, and Alternate Word on a separate index card. Indicate on each card whether a word is a Heart, Target, Challenge, or Alternate Word.

Pretest

1. **Administer** a pretest using the Heart and Target Words.

2. **Gather** students' Words to Learn cards.

Note: If students didn't misspell any Heart, Target, Challenge, or Alternate Words, mark Lessons 2 and 3 complete and move to the online activity for Day 4 to practice for the Unit Checkpoint on Day 5.

Heart Words

➲ *Skip this activity if students didn't misspell any Heart Words on this unit's pretest.*

1. **Gather** the Words to Learn cards for any Heart Words.

2. **Practice** the *new* Heart Words.

3. **Practice** *all* Heart Words.

4. **Track mastery** of Heart Words.

Target Words

➲ *Skip this activity if students didn't misspell any Target Words on this unit's pretest.*

1. **Gather** the Words to Learn cards for any Target Words.

2. **Discover** the new spelling convention.

3. **Practice** the Target Words.

Challenge Words

⮑ *Skip this activity if students are struggling with the Heart Words and Target Words.*

1. **Gather** the Words to Learn cards for any Challenge Words.
2. **Discover** the new spelling convention in the Challenge Words.
3. **Practice** the Challenge Words.

Alternate Words

⮑ *Skip this activity if students don't have any Words to Learn cards for Alternate Words.*

1. **Gather** the Words to Learn cards for any Alternate Words.
2. **Discover** the new spelling convention in the Alternate Words.
3. **Practice** the Alternate Words.

Day 2 ....

Practice Spelling Words

Practice using the Activity Bank.

Day 3 ....

Practice Spelling Words

Practice using the Activity Bank.

Day 4 ....

Review Spelling Words

Review using the online activity.

[Offline] ⏱ 15 minutes

Unit Checkpoint

1. **Dictate** the Heart Words and Target Words.

2. **Check** students' answers.

3. **Review** the words students misspelled.

Rewards:

- If students scored 80 percent or above on the Unit Checkpoint, add a sticker to the Unit 17 box on students' My Accomplishments chart. If students scored under 80 percent, continue to practice the words that they missed and add a sticker to this unit once they have mastered the words.

- Help students find and play the online Spelling game, Spell 'n' Stack. Students should use level 1.

Review Heart Words, Long Vowel, and Double *o* & /ow/ Spellings

In this unit, students will review the spelling conventions and Heart Words they studied in the previous five units. Refer back to the Unit Plans of previous units for a detailed description of each spelling convention.

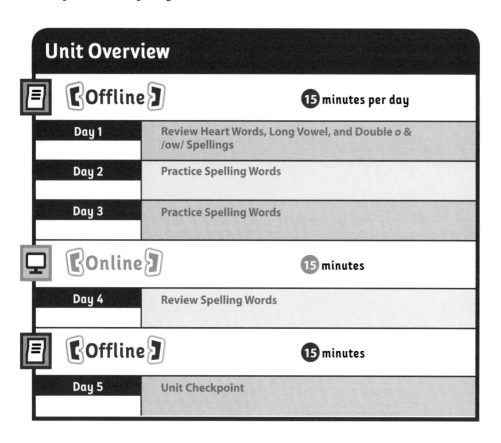

Unit Overview

📋 〖Offline〗   🕐 15 minutes per day

Day 1	Review Heart Words, Long Vowel, and Double *o* & /ow/ Spellings
Day 2	Practice Spelling Words
Day 3	Practice Spelling Words

🖥 〖Online〗   🕐 15 minutes

| Day 4 | Review Spelling Words |

📋 〖Offline〗   🕐 15 minutes

| Day 5 | Unit Checkpoint |

Objectives

- Spell Heart Words.
- Spell words containing the long *e* sound spelled *ee*, *ea*, *e*, or *e*-consonant-*e*.
- Spell words containing the long *e* sound spelled *ey* or *ie*.
- Spell words containing the long *u* sound spelled *ue*, *ew*, *u*, or *u*-consonant-*e*.
- Spell words containing the long double *o* sound spelled *ue*, *ew*, *oo*, or *u*-consonant-*e*.
- Spell words containing the short double *o* sound spelled *oo*.
- Spell words containing the sound /ow/ spelled *ou* or *ow*.

☁ Heart Words

eye	guest	knew
been	guard	shoe
where	guide	could
they	sure	would
guess	sew	should

◎ Target Words

dream	June	book
three	clue	ground
field	few	plow
unit	spool	stood
rescue		

★ Challenge Words

outboard	retrieve	balloon

Alternate Words

fear	yew	town
abbey	blew	

[Offline] ⏱ **15** minutes per day

Complete the Spelling activities with students. **For the full instructions for each activity, refer to pages SP 8–13.**

Day 1 ....

Review Heart Words, Long Vowel, and Double *o* & /ow/ Spellings

[Materials]

- index cards (8)
- whiteboard (optional)

Advance Preparation

Gather the index cards you made previously for the Heart and Target Words listed. Write each Challenge and Alternate Word on a separate index card. Indicate on each card whether a word is a Challenge or Alternate Word.

Pretest

1. **Administer** a pretest using the Heart and Target Words.

2. **Gather** students' Words to Learn cards.

Note: If students didn't misspell any Heart, Target, Challenge, or Alternate Words, mark Lessons 2 and 3 complete and move to the online activity for Day 4 to practice for the Unit Checkpoint on Day 5.

Heart Words

⮑ *Skip this activity if students didn't misspell any Heart Words on this unit's pretest.*

1. **Gather** the Words to Learn cards for any Heart Words.

2. **Practice** the Heart Words.

3. **Track mastery** of Heart Words.

Target Words

⮑ *Skip this activity if students didn't misspell any Target Words on this unit's pretest.*

1. **Gather** the Words to Learn cards for any Target Words.

2. **Review** the previously studied spelling convention in each Target Word.

3. **Practice** the Target Words.

Challenge Words

➲ *Skip this activity if students are struggling with the Heart Words and Target Words.*

1. **Gather** the Words to Learn cards for any Challenge Words.
2. **Review** the previously studied spelling convention in each Challenge Word.
3. **Practice** the Challenge Words.

Alternate Words

➲ *Skip this activity if students don't have any Words to Learn cards for Alternate Words.*

1. **Gather** the Words to Learn cards for any Alternate Words.
2. **Review** the previously studied spelling convention in each Alternate Word.
3. **Practice** the Alternate Words.

Day 2 ··

Practice Spelling Words

Practice using the Activity Bank.

Day 3 ··

Practice Spelling Words

Practice using the Activity Bank.

 **15** minutes

Day 4 ··

Review Spelling Words

Review using the online activity.

Day 5

Unit Checkpoint

1. **Dictate** the Heart Words and Target Words.

2. **Check** students' answers.

3. **Review** the words students misspelled.

Rewards:

- If students scored 80 percent or above on the Unit Checkpoint, add a sticker to the Unit 18 box on students' My Accomplishments chart. If students scored under 80 percent, continue to practice the words that they missed and add a sticker to this unit once they have mastered the words.

- Help students find and play the online Spelling game, Spell 'n' Stack. Students should use level 1.

Heart Words and /oi/ & /au/ Spellings

Target spelling convention – **letter combinations that create the sounds /oi/ and /au/**

We can spell the sound /oi/, as in the words *soil* and *joy*, with the letters *oi* or *oy* and the sound /au/, as in the words *law* and *haunt*, with the letters *aw* or *au*. This unit's Target Words contain the sound /oi/ spelled *oi* or *oy*, or the sound /au/ spelled *aw* or *au*.

> ⭐ **Objectives**
> - Spell Heart Words.
> - Spell words containing the sound /oi/ spelled *oi* or *oy*.
> - Spell words containing the sound /au/ spelled *aw* or *au*.

Unit Overview

🗎	**〖Offline〗**		⑮ minutes per day
Day 1	Introduce Heart Words and /oi/ & /au/ Spellings		
Day 2	Practice Spelling Words		
Day 3	Practice Spelling Words		

🖥	**〖Online〗**		⑮ minutes
Day 4	Review Spelling Words		

🗎	**〖Offline〗**		⑮ minutes
Day 5	Unit Checkpoint		

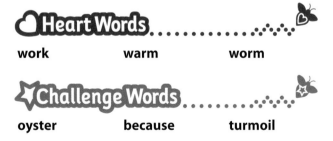
☁ Heart Words

work	warm	worm

✰ Challenge Words

oyster	because	turmoil

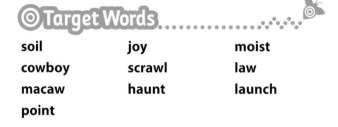
◎ Target Words

soil	joy	moist
cowboy	scrawl	law
macaw	haunt	launch
point		

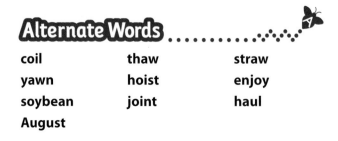
Alternate Words

coil	thaw	straw
yawn	hoist	enjoy
soybean	joint	haul
August		

Offline ⏱ 15 minutes per day

Complete the Spelling activities with students. **For the full instructions for each activity, refer to pages SP 8–13.**

Day 1

Introduce Heart Words and /oi/ & /au/ Spellings

Materials

- index cards (26)
- whiteboard (optional)

Advance Preparation

Write each Heart, Target, Challenge, and Alternate Word on a separate index card. Indicate on each card whether a word is a Heart, Target, Challenge, or Alternate Word.

Pretest

1. **Administer** a pretest using the Heart and Target Words.

2. **Gather** students' Words to Learn cards.

Note: If students didn't misspell any Heart, Target, Challenge, or Alternate Words, mark Lessons 2 and 3 complete and move to the online activity for Day 4 to practice for the Unit Checkpoint on Day 5.

Heart Words

⮑ *Skip this activity if students didn't misspell any Heart Words on this unit's pretest.*

1. **Gather** the Words to Learn cards for any Heart Words.

2. **Practice** the *new* Heart Words.

3. **Practice** *all* Heart Words.

4. **Track mastery** of Heart Words.

Target Words

⮑ *Skip this activity if students didn't misspell any Target Words on this unit's pretest.*

1. **Gather** the Words to Learn cards for any Target Words.

2. **Discover** the new spelling convention.

3. **Practice** the Target Words.

Challenge Words

➲ *Skip this activity if students are struggling with the Heart Words and Target Words.*

1. **Gather** the Words to Learn cards for any Challenge Words.
2. **Discover** the new spelling convention in the Challenge Words.
3. **Practice** the Challenge Words.

Alternate Words

➲ *Skip this activity if students don't have any Words to Learn cards for Alternate Words.*

1. **Gather** the Words to Learn cards for any Alternate Words.
2. **Discover** the new spelling convention in the Alternate Words.
3. **Practice** the Alternate Words.

Day 2

Practice Spelling Words

Practice using the Activity Bank.

Day 3

Practice Spelling Words

Practice using the Activity Bank.

 **15 minutes**

Day 4

Review Spelling Words

Review using the online activity.

[Offline] ⏱ **15** minutes

Day 5

Unit Checkpoint

1. **Dictate** the Heart Words and Target Words.

2. **Check** students' answers.

3. **Review** the words students misspelled.

Rewards:

- If students scored 80 percent or above on the Unit Checkpoint, add a sticker to the Unit 19 box on students' My Accomplishments chart. If students scored under 80 percent, continue to practice the words that they missed and add a sticker to this unit once they have mastered the words.

- Help students find and play the online Spelling game, Spell 'n' Stack. Students should use levels 1 and 2.

Heart Words and Long *e* & Long *i* Spelled *y*

Target spelling convention – **using the letter *y* to create long *i* or long *e* sounds**

When it appears at the end of a syllable, the letter *y* can have either the long *i* sound or the long *e* sound. Each of this unit's Target Words contains a syllable ending in *y*.

Objectives
- Spell Heart Words.
- Spell words containing the long *i* or long *e* sounds spelled with the letter *y*.

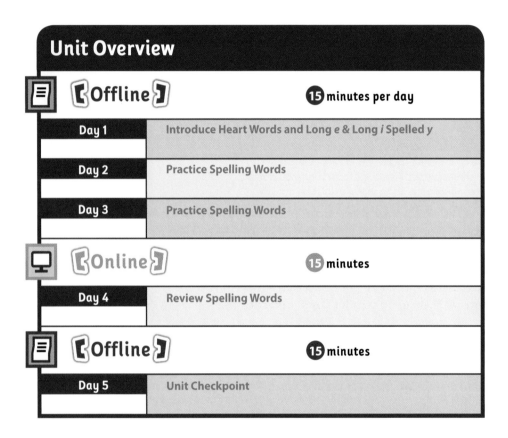

Unit Overview

【Offline】 🕐15 minutes per day

Day 1	Introduce Heart Words and Long *e* & Long *i* Spelled *y*
Day 2	Practice Spelling Words
Day 3	Practice Spelling Words

【Online】 🕐15 minutes

| Day 4 | Review Spelling Words |

【Offline】 🕐15 minutes

| Day 5 | Unit Checkpoint |

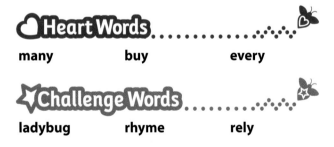

♡ Heart Words

| many | buy | every |

⭐ Challenge Words

| ladybug | rhyme | rely |

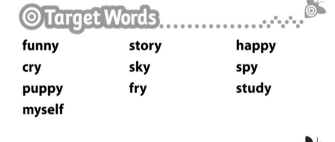

◎ Target Words

funny	story	happy
cry	sky	spy
puppy	fry	study
myself		

Alternate Words

bunny	babysit	shy
July	pretty	city
try	why	copy
dry		

[Offline] **15** minutes per day

Complete the Spelling activities with students. **For the full instructions for each activity, refer to pages SP 8–13.**

Day 1 ....

Introduce Heart Words and Long *e* & Long *i* Spelled *y*

[Materials]

- index cards (26)
- whiteboard (optional)

Advance Preparation

Write each Heart, Target, Challenge, and Alternate Word on a separate index card. Indicate on each card whether a word is a Heart, Target, Challenge, or Alternate Word.

Pretest

1. **Administer** a pretest using the Heart and Target Words.
2. **Gather** students' Words to Learn cards.

Note: If students didn't misspell any Heart, Target, Challenge, or Alternate Words, mark Lessons 2 and 3 complete and move to the online activity for Day 4 to practice for the Unit Checkpoint on Day 5.

Heart Words

➲ *Skip this activity if students didn't misspell any Heart Words on this unit's pretest.*

1. **Gather** the Words to Learn cards for any Heart Words.
2. **Practice** the *new* Heart Words.
3. **Practice** *all* Heart Words.
4. **Track mastery** of Heart Words.

Target Words

➲ *Skip this activity if students didn't misspell any Target Words on this unit's pretest.*

1. **Gather** the Words to Learn cards for any Target Words.
2. **Discover** the new spelling convention.
3. **Practice** the Target Words.

Challenge Words

➲ *Skip this activity if students are struggling with the Heart Words and Target Words.*

1. **Gather** the Words to Learn cards for any Challenge Words.
2. **Discover** the new spelling convention in the Challenge Words.
3. **Practice** the Challenge Words.

Alternate Words

➲ *Skip this activity if students don't have any Words to Learn cards for Alternate Words.*

1. **Gather** the Words to Learn cards for any Alternate Words.
2. **Discover** the new spelling convention in the Alternate Words.
3. **Practice** the Alternate Words.

Day 2 ....

Practice Spelling Words

Practice using the Activity Bank.

Day 3 ....

Practice Spelling Words

Practice using the Activity Bank.

 **15 minutes**

Day 4 ....

Review Spelling Words

Review using the online activity.

[Offline] 🕐 minutes

Day 5

Unit Checkpoint

1. **Dictate** the Heart Words and Target Words.

2. **Check** students' answers.

3. **Review** the words students misspelled.

Rewards:

- If students scored 80 percent or above on the Unit Checkpoint, add a sticker to the Unit 20 box on students' My Accomplishments chart. If students scored under 80 percent, continue to practice the words that they missed and add a sticker to this unit once they have mastered the words.

- Help students find and play the online Spelling game, Spell 'n' Stack. Students should use levels 1 and 2.

Heart Words and Closed Syllables

Target spelling convention — syllables with one short vowel sound that end with a consonant or consonants

When a syllable contains one short vowel sound and ends in one or more consonants, we call it a closed syllable. Each of this unit's Target Words is made up of two closed syllables.

Objectives
- Spell Heart Words.
- Spell words containing closed syllables.

Unit Overview

📄 【Offline】 ⑮ minutes per day

Day 1	Introduce Heart Words and Closed Syllables
Day 2	Practice Spelling Words
Day 3	Practice Spelling Words

🖥 【Online】 ⑮ minutes

Day 4	Review Spelling Words

📄 【Offline】 ⑮ minutes

Day 5	Unit Checkpoint

☁ Heart Words

through	though	thought

⭐ Challenge Words

Atlantic	fantastic	unselfish

◎ Target Words

cobweb	rabbit	sunset
suntan	picnic	sandbox
robin	basket	itself
napkin		

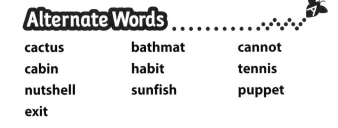

Alternate Words

cactus	bathmat	cannot
cabin	habit	tennis
nutshell	sunfish	puppet
exit		

 **15** minutes per day

Complete the Spelling activities with students. **For the full instructions for each activity, refer to pages SP 8–13.**

Day 1 ....

Introduce Heart Words and Closed Syllables

• index cards (26)
• whiteboard (optional)

Advance Preparation

Write each Heart, Target, Challenge, and Alternate Word on a separate index card. Indicate on each card whether a word is a Heart, Target, Challenge, or Alternate Word.

Pretest

1. **Administer** a pretest using the Heart and Target Words.

2. **Gather** students' Words to Learn cards.

Note: If students didn't misspell any Heart, Target, Challenge, or Alternate Words, mark Lessons 2 and 3 complete and move to the online activity for Day 4 to practice for the Unit Checkpoint on Day 5.

Heart Words

➲ *Skip this activity if students didn't misspell any Heart Words on this unit's pretest.*

1. **Gather** the Words to Learn cards for any Heart Words.

2. **Practice** the *new* Heart Words.

3. **Practice** *all* Heart Words.

4. **Track mastery** of Heart Words.

Target Words

➲ *Skip this activity if students didn't misspell any Target Words on this unit's pretest.*

1. **Gather** the Words to Learn cards for any Target Words.

2. **Discover** the new spelling convention.

3. **Practice** the Target Words.

Challenge Words

➲ *Skip this activity if students are struggling with the Heart Words and Target Words.*

1. **Gather** the Words to Learn cards for any Challenge Words.

2. **Discover** the new spelling convention in the Challenge Words.

3. **Practice** the Challenge Words.

Alternate Words

➲ *Skip this activity if students don't have any Words to Learn cards for Alternate Words.*

1. **Gather** the Words to Learn cards for any Alternate Words.

2. **Discover** the new spelling convention in the Alternate Words.

3. **Practice** the Alternate Words.

Day 2 ....

Practice Spelling Words

Practice using the Activity Bank.

Day 3 ....

Practice Spelling Words

Practice using the Activity Bank.

 **15 minutes**

Day 4 ....

Review Spelling Words

Review using the online activity.

⟦ Offline ⟧ ⑮ minutes

Day 5

Unit Checkpoint

1. **Dictate** the Heart Words and Target Words.

2. **Check** students' answers.

3. **Review** the words students misspelled.

Rewards:

- If students scored 80 percent or above on the Unit Checkpoint, add a sticker to the Unit 21 box on students' My Accomplishments chart. If students scored under 80 percent, continue to practice the words that they missed and add a sticker to this unit once they have mastered the words.

- Help students find and play the online Spelling game, Spell 'n' Stack. Students should use levels 1 and 2.

Heart Words and Open & Closed Syllables

Target spelling convention — **syllables ending in vowels; syllables with one short vowel sound that end with a consonant or consonants**

When a syllable ends in a vowel (usually with the long vowel sound), we call it an open syllable. Each of this unit's Target Words begins with an open syllable and ends with a closed syllable.

Unit Overview

📄 【Offline】 ⏱️ 15 minutes per day

Day 1	Introduce Heart Words and Open & Closed Syllables
Day 2	Practice Spelling Words
Day 3	Practice Spelling Words

🖥️ 【Online】 ⏱️ 15 minutes

Day 4	Review Spelling Words

📄 【Offline】 ⏱️ 15 minutes

Day 5	Unit Checkpoint

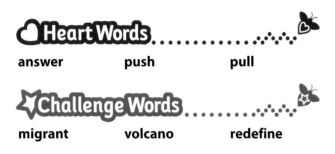

Heart Words

answer	push	pull

Challenge Words

migrant	volcano	redefine

Target Words

basin	tulip	respect
moment	frozen	pretend
open	secret	begin
protect		

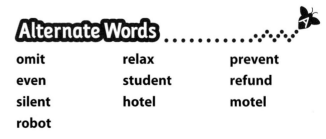

Alternate Words

omit	relax	prevent
even	student	refund
silent	hotel	motel
robot		

[Offline] 🕔 minutes per day

Complete the Spelling activities with students. **For the full instructions for each activity, refer to pages SP 8–13.**

Day 1

Introduce Heart Words and Open & Closed Syllables

[Materials]

- index cards (26)
- whiteboard (optional)

Advance Preparation

Write each Heart, Target, Challenge, and Alternate Word on a separate index card. Indicate on each card whether a word is a Heart, Target, Challenge, or Alternate Word.

Pretest

1. **Administer** a pretest using the Heart and Target Words.

2. **Gather** students' Words to Learn cards.

Note: If students didn't misspell any Heart, Target, Challenge, or Alternate Words, mark Lessons 2 and 3 complete and move to the online activity for Day 4 to practice for the Unit Checkpoint on Day 5.

Heart Words

➲ *Skip this activity if students didn't misspell any Heart Words on this unit's pretest.*

1. **Gather** the Words to Learn cards for any Heart Words.

2. **Practice** the *new* Heart Words.

3. **Practice** *all* Heart Words.

4. **Track mastery** of Heart Words.

Target Words

➲ *Skip this activity if students didn't misspell any Target Words on this unit's pretest.*

1. **Gather** the Words to Learn cards for any Target Words.

2. **Discover** the new spelling convention.

3. **Practice** the Target Words.

Challenge Words

➲ *Skip this activity if students are struggling with the Heart Words and Target Words.*

1. **Gather** the Words to Learn cards for any Challenge Words.
2. **Discover** the new spelling convention in the Challenge Words.
3. **Practice** the Challenge Words.

Alternate Words

➲ *Skip this activity if students don't have any Words to Learn cards for Alternate Words.*

1. **Gather** the Words to Learn cards for any Alternate Words.
2. **Discover** the new spelling convention in the Alternate Words.
3. **Practice** the Alternate Words.

Day 2 ....

Practice Spelling Words

Practice using the Activity Bank.

Day 3 ....

Practice Spelling Words

Practice using the Activity Bank.

 **minutes**

Day 4 ....

Review Spelling Words

Review using the online activity.

[Offline] 15 minutes

Day 5

Unit Checkpoint

1. **Dictate** the Heart Words and Target Words.
2. **Check** students' answers.
3. **Review** the words students misspelled.

Rewards:

- If students scored 80 percent or above on the Unit Checkpoint, add a sticker to the Unit 22 box on students' My Accomplishments chart. If students scored under 80 percent, continue to practice the words that they missed and add a sticker to this unit once they have mastered the words.
- Help students find and play the online Spelling game, Spell 'n' Stack. Students should use levels 1 and 2.

Heart Words and *v-c-e* Syllables

Target spelling convention – syllables containing a vowel + a consonant + *e*

When a syllable contains a vowel followed by a consonant and then the letter *e*, we call it a vowel-consonant-*e* (or *v-c-e*) syllable. Each of this unit's Target Words contains at least one vowel-consonant-*e* syllable.

Objectives
- Spell Heart Words.
- Spell words containing *v-c-e* syllables.

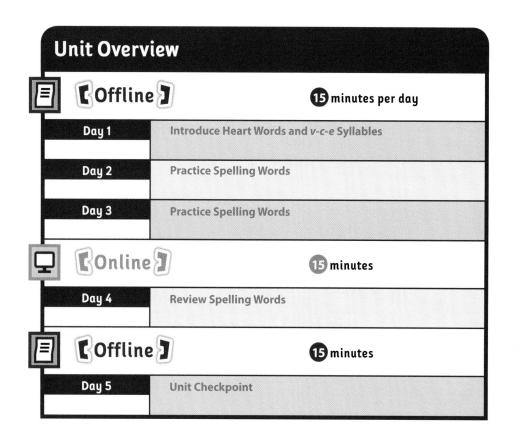

Unit Overview

Offline   15 minutes per day

Day 1	Introduce Heart Words and *v-c-e* Syllables
Day 2	Practice Spelling Words
Day 3	Practice Spelling Words

Online   15 minutes

| Day 4 | Review Spelling Words |

Offline   15 minutes

| Day 5 | Unit Checkpoint |

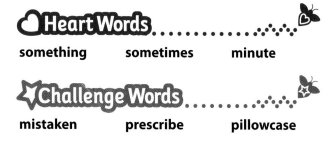

Heart Words

| something | sometimes | minute |

Challenge Words

| mistaken | prescribe | pillowcase |

Target Words

sunrise	inflate	behave
cupcake	inside	polite
snakeskin	athlete	skyline
racetrack		

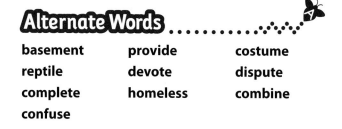

Alternate Words

basement	provide	costume
reptile	devote	dispute
complete	homeless	combine
confuse		

[Offline] ⏱ **15** minutes per day

Complete the Spelling activities with students. **For the full instructions for each activity, refer to pages SP 8–13.**

Day 1 ....

Introduce Heart Words and *v-c-e* Syllables

[Materials]

- index cards (26)
- whiteboard (optional)

Advance Preparation

Write each Heart, Target, Challenge, and Alternate Word on a separate index card. Indicate on each card whether a word is a Heart, Target, Challenge, or Alternate Word.

Pretest

1. **Administer** a pretest using the Heart and Target Words.

2. **Gather** students' Words to Learn cards.

Note: If students didn't misspell any Heart, Target, Challenge, or Alternate Words, mark Lessons 2 and 3 complete and move to the online activity for Day 4 to practice for the Unit Checkpoint on Day 5.

Heart Words

➲ *Skip this activity if students didn't misspell any Heart Words on this unit's pretest.*

1. **Gather** the Words to Learn cards for any Heart Words.

2. **Practice** the *new* Heart Words.

3. **Practice** *all* Heart Words.

4. **Track mastery** of Heart Words.

Target Words

➲ *Skip this activity if students didn't misspell any Target Words on this unit's pretest.*

1. **Gather** the Words to Learn cards for any Target Words.

2. **Discover** the new spelling convention.

3. **Practice** the Target Words.

Challenge Words

➲ *Skip this activity if students are struggling with the Heart Words and Target Words.*

1. **Gather** the Words to Learn cards for any Challenge Words.
2. **Discover** the new spelling convention in the Challenge Words.
3. **Practice** the Challenge Words.

Alternate Words

➲ *Skip this activity if students don't have any Words to Learn cards for Alternate Words.*

1. **Gather** the Words to Learn cards for any Alternate Words.
2. **Discover** the new spelling convention in the Alternate Words.
3. **Practice** the Alternate Words.

Day 2 ·

Practice Spelling Words

Practice using the Activity Bank.

Day 3 ·

Practice Spelling Words

Practice using the Activity Bank.

 **15 minutes**

Day 4 ·

Review Spelling Words

Review using the online activity.

Day 5

Unit Checkpoint

1. **Dictate** the Heart Words and Target Words.

2. **Check** students' answers.

3. **Review** the words students misspelled.

Rewards:

- If students scored 80 percent or above on the Unit Checkpoint, add a sticker to the Unit 23 box on students' My Accomplishments chart. If students scored under 80 percent, continue to practice the words that they missed and add a sticker to this unit once they have mastered the words.

- Help students find and play the online Spelling game, Spell 'n' Stack. Students should use levels 1 and 2.

Review Heart Words, /oi/, /au/, Long Vowels, and Closed & Open Syllables

In this unit, students will review the spelling conventions and Heart Words they studied in the previous five units. Refer back to the Unit Plans of previous units for a detailed description of each spelling convention.

Objectives

- Spell Heart Words.
- Spell words containing the sound /oi/ spelled *oi* or *oy*.
- Spell words containing the sound /au/ spelled *aw* or *au*.
- Spell words containing the long *i* or long *e* sounds spelled with the letter *y*.
- Spell words containing closed syllables.
- Spell words containing open syllables.
- Spell words containing *v-c-e* syllables.

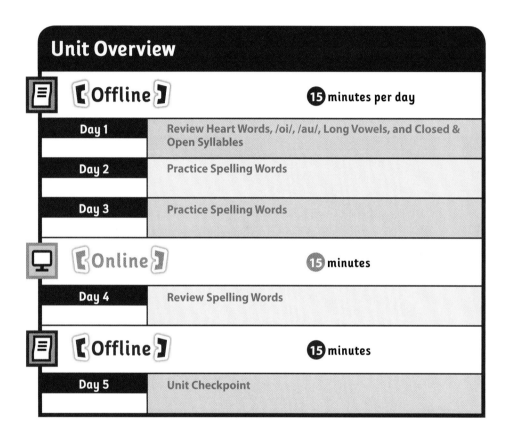

Unit Overview

Offline — 15 minutes per day

Day 1	Review Heart Words, /oi/, /au/, Long Vowels, and Closed & Open Syllables
Day 2	Practice Spelling Words
Day 3	Practice Spelling Words

Online — 15 minutes

| Day 4 | Review Spelling Words |

Offline — 15 minutes

| Day 5 | Unit Checkpoint |

♥ Heart Words

work	every	push
warm	through	pull
worm	though	something
many	thought	sometimes
buy	answer	minute

◎ Target Words

point	sky	sunrise
cowboy	cobweb	cupcake
macaw	sandbox	pretend
law	frozen	itself
funny		

☆ Challenge Words

therapy	demonstrate	misunderstood

Alternate Words

boil	bathtub	divide
ferry	prevent	

[Offline] ⓯ minutes per day

Complete the Spelling activities with students. **For the full instructions for each activity, refer to pages SP 8–13.**

Day 1

Review Heart Words, /oi/, /au/, Long Vowels, and Closed & Open Syllables

[Materials]

- index cards (8)
- whiteboard (optional)

Advance Preparation

Gather the index cards you made previously for the Heart and Target Words listed. Write each Challenge and Alternate Word on a separate index card. Indicate on each card whether a word is a Challenge or Alternate Word.

Pretest

1. **Administer** a pretest using the Heart and Target Words.

2. **Gather** students' Words to Learn cards.

Note: If students didn't misspell any Heart, Target, Challenge, or Alternate Words, mark Lessons 2 and 3 complete and move to the online activity for Day 4 to practice for the Unit Checkpoint on Day 5.

Heart Words

➲ *Skip this activity if students didn't misspell any Heart Words on this unit's pretest.*

1. **Gather** the Words to Learn cards for any Heart Words.

2. **Practice** the Heart Words.

3. **Track mastery** of Heart Words.

Target Words

➲ *Skip this activity if students didn't misspell any Target Words on this unit's pretest.*

1. **Gather** the Words to Learn cards for any Target Words.

2. **Review** the previously studied spelling convention in each Target Word.

3. **Practice** the Target Words.

Challenge Words

➲ *Skip this activity if students are struggling with the Heart Words and Target Words.*

1. **Gather** the Words to Learn cards for any Challenge Words.
2. **Review** the previously studied spelling convention in each Challenge Word.
3. **Practice** the Challenge Words.

Alternate Words

➲ *Skip this activity if students don't have any Words to Learn cards for Alternate Words.*

1. **Gather** the Words to Learn cards for any Alternate Words.
2. **Review** the previously studied spelling convention in each Alternate Word.
3. **Practice** the Alternate Words.

Day 2

Practice Spelling Words

Practice using the Activity Bank.

Day 3

Practice Spelling Words

Practice using the Activity Bank.

 **15 minutes**

Day 4

Review Spelling Words

Review using the online activity.

 **15** minutes

Day 5

Unit Checkpoint

1. **Dictate** the Heart Words and Target Words.

2. **Check** students' answers.

3. **Review** the words students misspelled.

 Rewards:

- If students scored 80 percent or above on the Unit Checkpoint, add a sticker to the Unit 24 box on students' My Accomplishments chart. If students scored under 80 percent, continue to practice the words that they missed and add a sticker to this unit once they have mastered the words.

- Help students find and play the online Spelling game, Spell 'n' Stack. Students should use levels 1 and 2.

Heart Words and Prefixes

Target spelling convention – **words beginning with *re–*, *sub–*, *un–*, *de–*, and *pre–***

A prefix is a word part that is added to the beginning of a base word and that changes the base word's meaning, but usually not its spelling. Each of this unit's Target Words begins with the prefix *re–*, *sub–*, *un–*, *de–*, or *pre–*.

Objectives
- Spell Heart Words.
- Spell words beginning with the prefixes *re–*, *sub–*, *un–*, *de–*, or *pre–*.

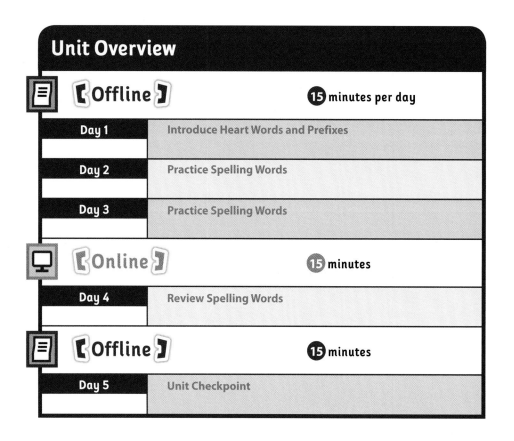

Unit Overview

⟦Offline⟧ 🔵 **15 minutes per day**

Day 1	Introduce Heart Words and Prefixes
Day 2	Practice Spelling Words
Day 3	Practice Spelling Words

⟦Online⟧ 🔵 **15 minutes**

| Day 4 | Review Spelling Words |

⟦Offline⟧ 🔵 **15 minutes**

| Day 5 | Unit Checkpoint |

Heart Words

| tough | rough | cough |

Challenge Words

| department | undressing | substandard |

Target Words

rebuild	subway	prefix
remind	subscribe	unfair
depart	preheat	untie
depress		

Alternate Words

report	describe	unkind
pretend	unsafe	subzero
recall	depend	unzip
prevent		

[Offline] ⏱ minutes per day

Complete the Spelling activities with students. **For the full instructions for each activity, refer to pages SP 8–13.**

Day 1
Introduce Heart Words and Prefixes

[Materials]

- index cards (26)
- whiteboard (optional)

Advance Preparation

Write each Heart, Target, Challenge, and Alternate Word on a separate index card. Indicate on each card whether a word is a Heart, Target, Challenge, or Alternate Word.

Pretest

1. **Administer** a pretest using the Heart and Target Words.

2. **Gather** students' Words to Learn cards.

Note: If students didn't misspell any Heart, Target, Challenge, or Alternate Words, mark Lessons 2 and 3 complete and move to the online activity for Day 4 to practice for the Unit Checkpoint on Day 5.

Heart Words

➲ *Skip this activity if students didn't misspell any Heart Words on this unit's pretest.*

1. **Gather** the Words to Learn cards for any Heart Words.

2. **Practice** the *new* Heart Words.

3. **Practice** *all* Heart Words.

4. **Track mastery** of Heart Words.

Target Words

➲ *Skip this activity if students didn't misspell any Target Words on this unit's pretest.*

1. **Gather** the Words to Learn cards for any Target Words.

2. **Discover** the new spelling convention.

3. **Practice** the Target Words.

Challenge Words

➲ *Skip this activity if students are struggling with the Heart Words and Target Words.*

1. **Gather** the Words to Learn cards for any Challenge Words.
2. **Discover** the new spelling convention in the Challenge Words.
3. **Practice** the Challenge Words.

Alternate Words

➲ *Skip this activity if students don't have any Words to Learn cards for Alternate Words.*

1. **Gather** the Words to Learn cards for any Alternate Words.
2. **Discover** the new spelling convention in the Alternate Words.
3. **Practice** the Alternate Words.

Day 2 ....

Practice Spelling Words

Practice using the Activity Bank.

Day 3 ....

Practice Spelling Words

Practice using the Activity Bank.

 **15 minutes**

Day 4 ....

Review Spelling Words

Review using the online activity.

 **[Offline]** ⏱ **15** minutes

Day 5

Unit Checkpoint

1. **Dictate** the Heart Words and Target Words.

2. **Check** students' answers.

3. **Review** the words students misspelled.

 Rewards:

- If students scored 80 percent or above on the Unit Checkpoint, add a sticker to the Unit 25 box on students' My Accomplishments chart. If students scored under 80 percent, continue to practice the words that they missed and add a sticker to this unit once they have mastered the words.

- Help students find and play the online Spelling game, Spell 'n' Stack. Students should use levels 1 and 2.

Heart Words and Consonant Suffixes (A)

Target spelling convention – **words ending in –*ly*, –*ful*, –*fully*, –*ment*, –*less*, –*ness*, –*ty*, and –*some***

A suffix is a word part that is added to the end of a base word and that changes the base word's meaning. A suffix can also sometimes change the spelling of the base word. Each of this unit's Target Words ends with the consonant suffix –*ly*, –*ful*, –*fully*, –*ment*, –*less*, –*ness*, –*ty*, or –*some*.

Objectives
- Spell Heart Words.
- Spell words ending with the consonant suffixes –*ly*, –*ful*, –*fully*, –*ment*, –*less*, –*ness*, –*ty*, or –*some*.

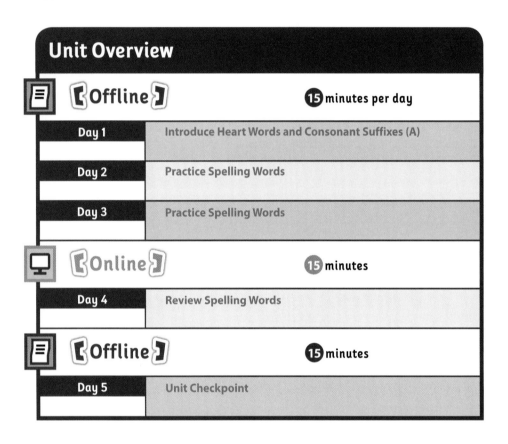

Unit Overview

[Offline]		⑮ minutes per day
Day 1	Introduce Heart Words and Consonant Suffixes (A)	
Day 2	Practice Spelling Words	
Day 3	Practice Spelling Words	
[Online]		⑮ minutes
Day 4	Review Spelling Words	
[Offline]		⑮ minutes
Day 5	Unit Checkpoint	

Heart Words

month	ninth	love

Challenge Words

amendment	awesome	forgetfully

Target Words

quickly	truthfully	ninety
safely	weakness	handsome
faithful	blameless	payment
cheerful		

Alternate Words

gladly	thankful	sixty
darkness	safety	playfully
lonesome	hopeful	shipment
helpless		

[Offline] 🕔 minutes per day

Complete the Spelling activities with students. **For the full instructions for each activity, refer to pages SP 8–13.**

Day 1 ....

Introduce Heart Words and Consonant Suffixes (A)

Advance Preparation

Write each Heart, Target, Challenge, and Alternate Word on a separate index card. Indicate on each card whether a word is a Heart, Target, Challenge, or Alternate Word.

[Materials]

- index cards (26)
- whiteboard (optional)

Pretest

1. **Administer** a pretest using the Heart and Target Words.

2. **Gather** students' Words to Learn cards.

Note: If students didn't misspell any Heart, Target, Challenge, or Alternate Words, mark Lessons 2 and 3 complete and move to the online activity for Day 4 to practice for the Unit Checkpoint on Day 5.

Heart Words

⟳ *Skip this activity if students didn't misspell any Heart Words on this unit's pretest.*

1. **Gather** the Words to Learn cards for any Heart Words.

2. **Practice** the *new* Heart Words.

3. **Practice** *all* Heart Words.

4. **Track mastery** of Heart Words.

Target Words

⟳ *Skip this activity if students didn't misspell any Target Words on this unit's pretest.*

1. **Gather** the Words to Learn cards for any Target Words.

2. **Discover** the new spelling convention.

3. **Practice** the Target Words.

Challenge Words

↪ *Skip this activity if students are struggling with the Heart Words and Target Words.*

1. **Gather** the Words to Learn cards for any Challenge Words.

2. **Discover** the new spelling convention in the Challenge Words.

3. **Practice** the Challenge Words.

Alternate Words

↪ *Skip this activity if students don't have any Words to Learn cards for Alternate Words.*

1. **Gather** the Words to Learn cards for any Alternate Words.

2. **Discover** the new spelling convention in the Alternate Words.

3. **Practice** the Alternate Words.

Day 2 ....

Practice Spelling Words

Practice using the Activity Bank.

Day 3 ....

Practice Spelling Words

Practice using the Activity Bank.

 **15 minutes**

Day 4 ....

Review Spelling Words

Review using the online activity.

[Offline] ⓯ minutes

Day 5

Unit Checkpoint

1. **Dictate** the Heart Words and Target Words.

2. **Check** students' answers.

3. **Review** the words students misspelled.

Rewards:

- If students scored 80 percent or above on the Unit Checkpoint, add a sticker to the Unit 26 box on students' My Accomplishments chart. If students scored under 80 percent, continue to practice the words that they missed and add a sticker to this unit once they have mastered the words.

- Help students find and play the online Spelling game, Spell 'n' Stack. Students should use levels 1 and 2.

Heart Words and Vowel Suffixes (A)

Target spelling convention — words ending in _–able_, _–en_, _–est_, _–ish_, and _–y_

When suffixes begin with vowels, we call them vowel suffixes. Vowel suffixes do not change the spelling of base words that end in consonants. Vowel suffixes do change the spelling of some base words that end in vowels. Each of this unit's Target Words ends in the vowel suffix _–able_, _–en_, _–est_, _–ish_, or _–y_.

Objectives
- Spell Heart Words.
- Spell words ending with the vowel suffixes _–able_, _–en_, _–est_, _–ish_, or _–y_.

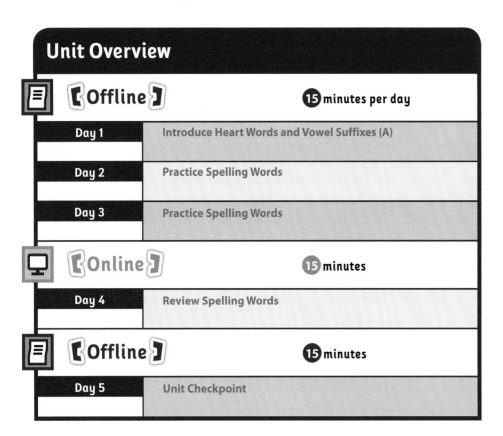

Unit Overview

Offline — 15 minutes per day

Day 1	Introduce Heart Words and Vowel Suffixes (A)
Day 2	Practice Spelling Words
Day 3	Practice Spelling Words

Online — 15 minutes

| Day 4 | Review Spelling Words |

Offline — 15 minutes

| Day 5 | Unit Checkpoint |

Heart Words

laugh   island   touch

Challenge Words

agreeable   healthy   cartoonish

Target Words

oldest	breakable	foolish
longest	predictable	cloudy
dampen	selfish	tricky
brighten		

Alternate Words

greatest	golden	rainy
dependable	girlish	enjoyable
strongest	shorten	snowy
childish		

Offline ⏱ **15** minutes per day

Complete the Spelling activities with students. **For the full instructions for each activity, refer to pages SP 8–13.**

Day 1

Introduce Heart Words and Vowel Suffixes (A)

〔 Materials 〕

- index cards (26)
- whiteboard (optional)

Advance Preparation

Write each Heart, Target, Challenge, and Alternate Word on a separate index card. Indicate on each card whether a word is a Heart, Target, Challenge, or Alternate Word.

Pretest

1. **Administer** a pretest using the Heart and Target Words.

2. **Gather** students' Words to Learn cards.

Note: If students didn't misspell any Heart, Target, Challenge, or Alternate Words, mark Lessons 2 and 3 complete and move to the online activity for Day 4 to practice for the Unit Checkpoint on Day 5.

Heart Words

➲ *Skip this activity if students didn't misspell any Heart Words on this unit's pretest.*

1. **Gather** the Words to Learn cards for any Heart Words.

2. **Practice** the *new* Heart Words.

3. **Practice** *all* Heart Words.

4. **Track mastery** of Heart Words.

Target Words

➲ *Skip this activity if students didn't misspell any Target Words on this unit's pretest.*

1. **Gather** the Words to Learn cards for any Target Words.

2. **Discover** the new spelling convention.

3. **Practice** the Target Words.

Challenge Words

⮑ *Skip this activity if students are struggling with the Heart Words and Target Words.*

1. **Gather** the Words to Learn cards for any Challenge Words.
2. **Discover** the new spelling convention in the Challenge Words.
3. **Practice** the Challenge Words.

Alternate Words

⮑ *Skip this activity if students don't have any Words to Learn cards for Alternate Words.*

1. **Gather** the Words to Learn cards for any Alternate Words.
2. **Discover** the new spelling convention in the Alternate Words.
3. **Practice** the Alternate Words.

Day 2 ....

Practice Spelling Words

Practice using the Activity Bank.

Day 3 ....

Practice Spelling Words

Practice using the Activity Bank.

[Online] 15 minutes

Day 4 ....

Review Spelling Words

Review using the online activity.

[Offline] ⑮ minutes

Unit Checkpoint

1. **Dictate** the Heart Words and Target Words.

2. **Check** students' answers.

3. **Review** the words students misspelled.

Rewards:

- If students scored 80 percent or above on the Unit Checkpoint, add a sticker to the Unit 27 box on students' My Accomplishments chart. If students scored under 80 percent, continue to practice the words that they missed and add a sticker to this unit once they have mastered the words.

- Help students find and play the online Spelling game, Spell 'n' Stack. Students should use levels 1 and 2.

Heart Words and Multisyllabic Words with *r*-Controlled Vowels

Target spelling convention — the sounds of short vowels followed by the letter *r* in multisyllabic words

Short vowels are pronounced differently when followed by the letter *r*. They are *r*-controlled vowels. Each Target Word has two syllables and at least one *r*-controlled vowel.

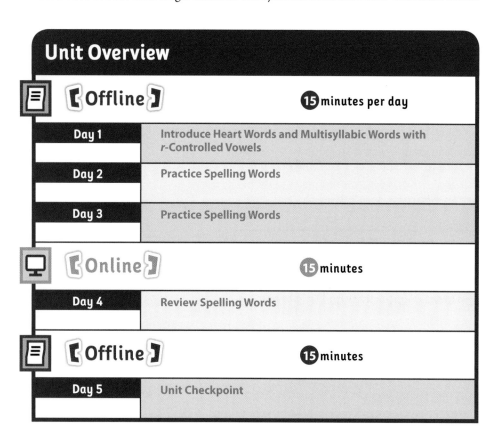

Unit Overview

📋 **〖 Offline 〗** ⏱**15** minutes per day

Day 1	Introduce Heart Words and Multisyllabic Words with *r*-Controlled Vowels
Day 2	Practice Spelling Words
Day 3	Practice Spelling Words

🖥 **〖 Online 〗** ⏱**15** minutes

| Day 4 | Review Spelling Words |

📋 **〖 Offline 〗** ⏱**15** minutes

| Day 5 | Unit Checkpoint |

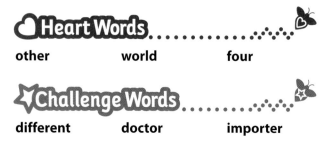

♡ Heart Words

| other | world | four |

☆ Challenge Words

| different | doctor | importer |

◎ Target Words

farmer	thirsty	perform
harvest	birthday	surprise
perhaps	corner	current
expert		

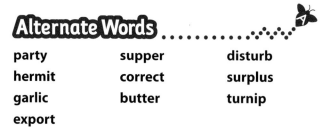

Alternate Words

party	supper	disturb
hermit	correct	surplus
garlic	butter	turnip
export		

[Offline] ⏱ 15 minutes per day

Complete the Spelling activities with students. **For the full instructions for each activity, refer to pages SP 8–13.**

Day 1 ·

Introduce Heart Words and Multisyllabic Words with *r*-Controlled Vowels

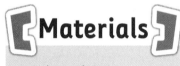

[Materials]

- index cards (26)
- whiteboard (optional)

Advance Preparation

Write each Heart, Target, Challenge, and Alternate Word on a separate index card. Indicate on each card whether a word is a Heart, Target, Challenge, or Alternate Word.

Pretest

1. **Administer** a pretest using the Heart and Target Words.
2. **Gather** students' Words to Learn cards.

Note: If students didn't misspell any Heart, Target, Challenge, or Alternate Words, mark Lessons 2 and 3 complete and move to the online activity for Day 4 to practice for the Unit Checkpoint on Day 5.

Heart Words

➲ *Skip this activity if students didn't misspell any Heart Words on this unit's pretest.*

1. **Gather** the Words to Learn cards for any Heart Words.
2. **Practice** the *new* Heart Words.
3. **Practice** *all* Heart Words.
4. **Track mastery** of Heart Words.

Target Words

➲ *Skip this activity if students didn't misspell any Target Words on this unit's pretest.*

1. **Gather** the Words to Learn cards for any Target Words.
2. **Discover** the new spelling convention.
3. **Practice** the Target Words.

Challenge Words

➲ *Skip this activity if students are struggling with the Heart Words and Target Words.*

1. **Gather** the Words to Learn cards for any Challenge Words.
2. **Discover** the new spelling convention in the Challenge Words.
3. **Practice** the Challenge Words.

Alternate Words

➲ *Skip this activity if students don't have any Words to Learn cards for Alternate Words.*

1. **Gather** the Words to Learn cards for any Alternate Words.
2. **Discover** the new spelling convention in the Alternate Words.
3. **Practice** the Alternate Words.

Day 2 ....

Practice Spelling Words
Practice using the Activity Bank.

Day 3 ....

Practice Spelling Words
Practice using the Activity Bank.

 **15 minutes**

Day 4 ....

Review Spelling Words
Review using the online activity.

[Offline] 🕐 **minutes**

Day 5

Unit Checkpoint

1. **Dictate** the Heart Words and Target Words.

2. **Check** students' answers.

3. **Review** the words students misspelled.

Rewards:

- If students scored 80 percent or above on the Unit Checkpoint, add a sticker to the Unit 28 box on students' My Accomplishments chart. If students scored under 80 percent, continue to practice the words that they missed and add a sticker to this unit once they have mastered the words.

- Help students find and play the online Spelling game, Spell 'n' Stack. Students should use levels 1 and 2.

Heart Words and Consonant-*le* Syllables

Target spelling convention — **syllables containing a consonant + *le***

When a word ends with a consonant-*le* syllable, the final *e* is always silent. Each of this unit's Target Words ends with a consonant-*le* syllable.

Objectives
- Spell Heart Words.
- Spell words containing consonant-*le* syllables.

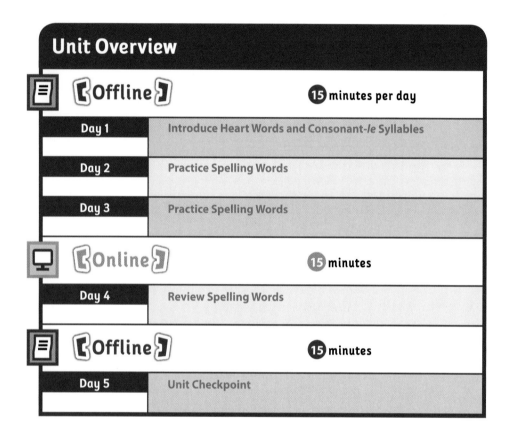

Unit Overview

▤ 〖Offline〗 🕔 15 minutes per day

Day 1	Introduce Heart Words and Consonant-*le* Syllables
Day 2	Practice Spelling Words
Day 3	Practice Spelling Words

🖥 〖Online〗 🕔 15 minutes

Day 4	Review Spelling Words

▤ 〖Offline〗 🕔 15 minutes

Day 5	Unit Checkpoint

☁ Heart Words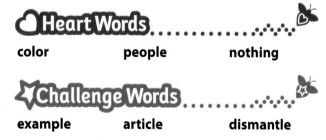

color	people	nothing

☆ Challenge Words

example	article	dismantle

◎ Target Words

apple	saddle	ruffle
turtle	maple	dazzle
table	tingle	bumble
ankle		

Alternate Words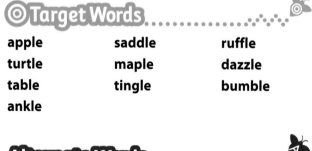

purple	marble	stable
simple	needle	huddle
cattle	sparkle	candle
jingle		

Offline ⏱ 15 minutes per day

Complete the Spelling activities with students. **For the full instructions for each activity, refer to pages SP 8–13.**

Day 1 ....

Introduce Heart Words and Consonant-*le* Syllables

Materials

- index cards (26)
- whiteboard (optional)

Advance Preparation

Write each Heart, Target, Challenge, and Alternate Word on a separate index card. Indicate on each card whether a word is a Heart, Target, Challenge, or Alternate Word.

Pretest

1. **Administer** a pretest using the Heart and Target Words.

2. **Gather** students' Words to Learn cards.

Note: If students didn't misspell any Heart, Target, Challenge, or Alternate Words, mark Lessons 2 and 3 complete and move to the online activity for Day 4 to practice for the Unit Checkpoint on Day 5.

Heart Words

➲ *Skip this activity if students didn't misspell any Heart Words on this unit's pretest.*

1. **Gather** the Words to Learn cards for any Heart Words.

2. **Practice** the *new* Heart Words.

3. **Practice** *all* Heart Words.

4. **Track mastery** of Heart Words.

Target Words

➲ *Skip this activity if students didn't misspell any Target Words on this unit's pretest.*

1. **Gather** the Words to Learn cards for any Target Words.

2. **Discover** the new spelling convention.

3. **Practice** the Target Words.

Challenge Words

⮑ *Skip this activity if students are struggling with the Heart Words and Target Words.*

1. **Gather** the Words to Learn cards for any Challenge Words.
2. **Discover** the new spelling convention in the Challenge Words.
3. **Practice** the Challenge Words.

Alternate Words

⮑ *Skip this activity if students don't have any Words to Learn cards for Alternate Words.*

1. **Gather** the Words to Learn cards for any Alternate Words.
2. **Discover** the new spelling convention in the Alternate Words.
3. **Practice** the Alternate Words.

Day 2 ....

Practice Spelling Words

Practice using the Activity Bank.

Day 3 ....

Practice Spelling Words

Practice using the Activity Bank.

 **15 minutes**

Day 4 ....

Review Spelling Words

Review using the online activity.

Offline ⏱ 15 minutes

Unit Checkpoint

1. **Dictate** the Heart Words and Target Words.

2. **Check** students' answers.

3. **Review** the words students misspelled.

Rewards:

- If students scored 80 percent or above on the Unit Checkpoint, add a sticker to the Unit 29 box on students' My Accomplishments chart. If students scored under 80 percent, continue to practice the words that they missed and add a sticker to this unit once they have mastered the words.

- Help students find and play the online Spelling game, Spell 'n' Stack. Students should use levels 1 and 2.

Review Heart Words, Prefixes, Suffixes, *r*-Controlled Vowels, and Consonant-*le* Syllables

In this unit, students will review the spelling conventions and Heart Words they studied in the previous five units. Refer back to the Unit Plans of previous units for a detailed description of each spelling convention.

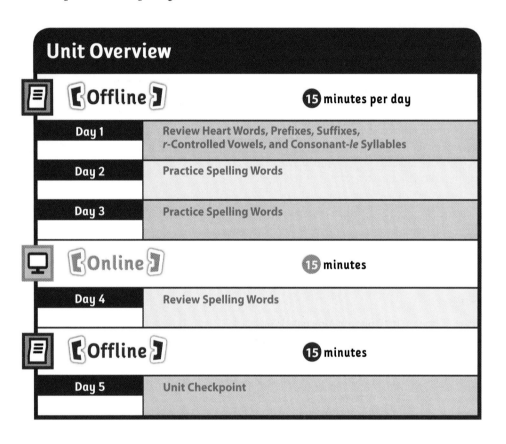

Unit Overview

	Offline	15 minutes per day
Day 1	Review Heart Words, Prefixes, Suffixes, *r*-Controlled Vowels, and Consonant-*le* Syllables	
Day 2	Practice Spelling Words	
Day 3	Practice Spelling Words	

	Online	15 minutes
Day 4	Review Spelling Words	

	Offline	15 minutes
Day 5	Unit Checkpoint	

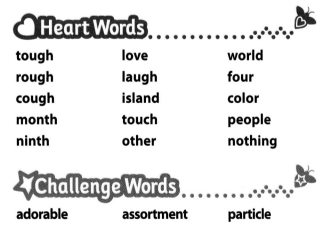

Heart Words

tough	love	world
rough	laugh	four
cough	island	color
month	touch	people
ninth	other	nothing

Challenge Words

adorable	assortment	particle

Target Words

rebuild	payment	farmer
depart	ankle	birthday
cheerful	oldest	turtle
quickly	selfish	bumble

Alternate Words

undo	dirty	muddle
clueless	harmful	

 **Offline** ⑮ minutes per day

Complete the Spelling activities with students. **For the full instructions for each activity, refer to pages SP 8–13.**

Day 1 ....

Review Heart Words, Prefixes, Suffixes, *r*-Controlled Vowels, and Consonant-*le* Syllables

 **Materials**

- index cards (8)
- whiteboard (optional)

Advance Preparation

Gather the index cards you made previously for the Heart and Target Words listed. Write each Challenge and Alternate Word on a separate index card. Indicate on each card whether a word is a Challenge or Alternate Word.

Pretest

1. **Administer** a pretest using the Heart and Target Words.

2. **Gather** students' Words to Learn cards.

Note: If students didn't misspell any Heart, Target, Challenge, or Alternate Words, mark Lessons 2 and 3 complete and move to the online activity for Day 4 to practice for the Unit Checkpoint on Day 5.

Heart Words

⊃ *Skip this activity if students didn't misspell any Heart Words on this unit's pretest.*

1. **Gather** the Words to Learn cards for any Heart Words.

2. **Practice** the Heart Words.

3. **Track mastery** of Heart Words.

Target Words

⊃ *Skip this activity if students didn't misspell any Target Words on this unit's pretest.*

1. **Gather** the Words to Learn cards for any Target Words.

2. **Review** the previously studied spelling convention in each Target Word.

3. **Practice** the Target Words.

Challenge Words

➲ *Skip this activity if students are struggling with the Heart Words and Target Words.*

1. **Gather** the Words to Learn cards for any Challenge Words.
2. **Review** the previously studied spelling convention in each Challenge Word.
3. **Practice** the Challenge Words.

Alternate Words

➲ *Skip this activity if students don't have any Words to Learn cards for Alternate Words.*

1. **Gather** the Words to Learn cards for any Alternate Words.
2. **Review** the previously studied spelling convention in each Alternate Word.
3. **Practice** the Alternate Words.

Day 2 ....

Practice Spelling Words

Practice using the Activity Bank.

Day 3 ....

Practice Spelling Words

Practice using the Activity Bank.

 15 minutes

Day 4 ....

Review Spelling Words

Review using the online activity.

 **[Offline]** **15** minutes

Day 5

Unit Checkpoint

1. **Dictate** the Heart Words and Target Words.

2. **Check** students' answers.

3. **Review** the words students misspelled.

 Rewards:

- If students scored 80 percent or above on the Unit Checkpoint, add a sticker to the Unit 30 box on students' My Accomplishments chart. If students scored under 80 percent, continue to practice the words that they missed and add a sticker to this unit once they have mastered the words.

- Help students find and play the online Spelling game, Spell 'n' Stack. Students should use levels 1 and 2.

Heart Words and Multisyllabic Words with Vowel-Team Syllables

Target spelling convention – **two letters that form one vowel sound in multisyllabic words**

We call two or more letters that form one vowel sound a vowel team. A syllable that has a vowel team is a vowel-team syllable. Each Target Word has at least one vowel-team syllable.

Objectives
- Spell Heart Words.
- Spell multisyllabic words containing vowel-team syllables.

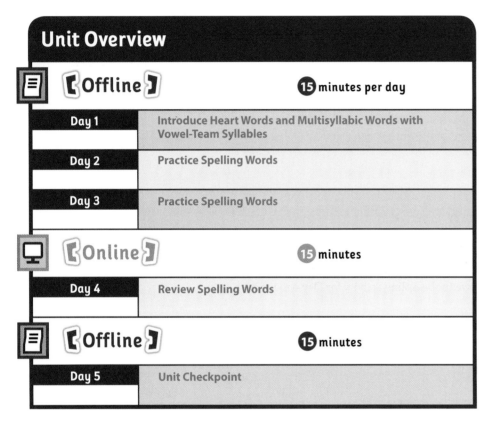

Unit Overview

▤ 〖Offline〗   🕔 **minutes per day**

Day 1	Introduce Heart Words and Multisyllabic Words with Vowel-Team Syllables
Day 2	Practice Spelling Words
Day 3	Practice Spelling Words

🖥 〖Online〗   🕔 **minutes**

| Day 4 | Review Spelling Words |

▤ 〖Offline〗   🕔 **minutes**

| Day 5 | Unit Checkpoint |

♥ Heart Words

| journey | flood | calf |

☆ Challenge Words

| eyebrow | delightful | concealment |

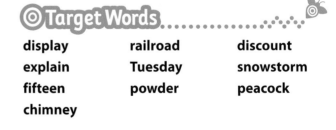

◎ Target Words

display	railroad	discount
explain	Tuesday	snowstorm
fifteen	powder	peacock
chimney		

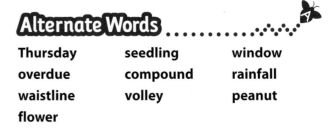

Alternate Words

Thursday	seedling	window
overdue	compound	rainfall
waistline	volley	peanut
flower		

[Offline] ⏱ 15 minutes per day

Complete the Spelling activities with students. **For the full instructions for each activity, refer to pages SP 8–13.**

Day 1 ....

Introduce Heart Words and Multisyllabic Words with Vowel-Team Syllables

[Materials]

- index cards (26)
- whiteboard (optional)

Advance Preparation

Write each Heart, Target, Challenge, and Alternate Word on a separate index card. Indicate on each card whether a word is a Heart, Target, Challenge, or Alternate Word.

Pretest

1. **Administer** a pretest using the Heart and Target Words.

2. **Gather** students' Words to Learn cards.

Note: If students didn't misspell any Heart, Target, Challenge, or Alternate Words, mark Lessons 2 and 3 complete and move to the online activity for Day 4 to practice for the Unit Checkpoint on Day 5.

Heart Words

⮑ *Skip this activity if students didn't misspell any Heart Words on this unit's pretest.*

1. **Gather** the Words to Learn cards for any Heart Words.

2. **Practice** the *new* Heart Words.

3. **Practice** *all* Heart Words.

4. **Track mastery** of Heart Words.

Target Words

⮑ *Skip this activity if students didn't misspell any Target Words on this unit's pretest.*

1. **Gather** the Words to Learn cards for any Target Words.

2. **Discover** the new spelling convention.

3. **Practice** the Target Words.

Challenge Words

➲ *Skip this activity if students are struggling with the Heart Words and Target Words.*

1. **Gather** the Words to Learn cards for any Challenge Words.
2. **Discover** the new spelling convention in the Challenge Words.
3. **Practice** the Challenge Words.

Alternate Words

➲ *Skip this activity if students don't have any Words to Learn cards for Alternate Words.*

1. **Gather** the Words to Learn cards for any Alternate Words.
2. **Discover** the new spelling convention in the Alternate Words.
3. **Practice** the Alternate Words.

Day 2 ....

Practice Spelling Words

Practice using the Activity Bank.

Day 3 ....

Practice Spelling Words

Practice using the Activity Bank.

 **minutes**

Day 4 ....

Review Spelling Words

Review using the online activity.

[Offline] ⑮ minutes

Unit Checkpoint

1. **Dictate** the Heart Words and Target Words.

2. **Check** students' answers.

3. **Review** the words students misspelled.

Rewards:

- If students scored 80 percent or above on the Unit Checkpoint, add a sticker to the Unit 31 box on students' My Accomplishments chart. If students scored under 80 percent, continue to practice the words that they missed and add a sticker to this unit once they have mastered the words.

- Help students find and play the online Spelling game, Spell 'n' Stack. Students should use levels 1 and 2.

Heart Words and Vowel Suffixes (B)

Target spelling convention — **words ending in –ed, –est, –ing, or –er**

We call a suffix that begins with a vowel a vowel suffix. Some base words that end in vowels change their spellings when vowel suffixes are added. Each of this unit's Target Words contains a base word that has changed its spelling when a vowel suffix was added.

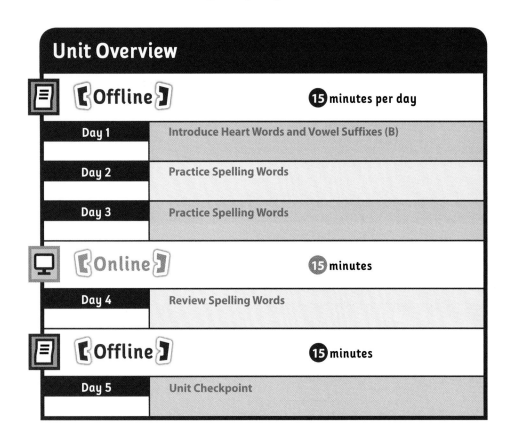

Unit Overview

Offline — 15 minutes per day

Day 1	Introduce Heart Words and Vowel Suffixes (B)
Day 2	Practice Spelling Words
Day 3	Practice Spelling Words

Online — 15 minutes

| Day 4 | Review Spelling Words |

Offline — 15 minutes

| Day 5 | Unit Checkpoint |

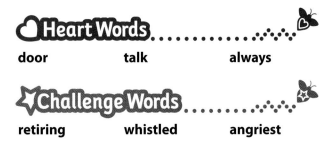

♡ Heart Words

| door | talk | always |

☆ Challenge Words

| retiring | whistled | angriest |

◎ Target Words

chased	easiest	hidden
filed	nicest	riper
sloping	tapping	starring
dancing		

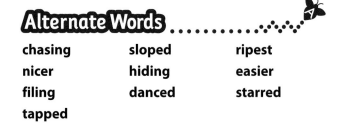

Alternate Words

chasing	sloped	ripest
nicer	hiding	easier
filing	danced	starred
tapped		

Offline ⏱ 15 minutes per day

Complete the Spelling activities with students. **For the full instructions for each activity, refer to pages SP 8–13.**

Day 1

Introduce Heart Words and Vowel Suffixes (B)

Materials

- index cards (26)
- whiteboard (optional)

Advance Preparation

Write each Heart, Target, Challenge, and Alternate Word on a separate index card. Indicate on each card whether a word is a Heart, Target, Challenge, or Alternate Word.

Pretest

1. **Administer** a pretest using the Heart and Target Words.

2. **Gather** students' Words to Learn cards.

Note: If students didn't misspell any Heart, Target, Challenge, or Alternate Words, mark Lessons 2 and 3 complete and move to the online activity for Day 4 to practice for the Unit Checkpoint on Day 5.

Heart Words

➲ *Skip this activity if students didn't misspell any Heart Words on this unit's pretest.*

1. **Gather** the Words to Learn cards for any Heart Words.

2. **Practice** the *new* Heart Words.

3. **Practice** *all* Heart Words.

4. **Track mastery** of Heart Words.

Target Words

➲ *Skip this activity if students didn't misspell any Target Words on this unit's pretest.*

1. **Gather** the Words to Learn cards for any Target Words.

2. **Discover** the new spelling convention.

3. **Practice** the Target Words.

Challenge Words

➲ *Skip this activity if students are struggling with the Heart Words and Target Words.*

1. **Gather** the Words to Learn cards for any Challenge Words.

2. **Discover** the new spelling convention in the Challenge Words.

3. **Practice** the Challenge Words.

Alternate Words

➲ *Skip this activity if students don't have any Words to Learn cards for Alternate Words.*

1. **Gather** the Words to Learn cards for any Alternate Words.

2. **Discover** the new spelling convention in the Alternate Words.

3. **Practice** the Alternate Words.

Day 2 ....

Practice Spelling Words

Practice using the Activity Bank.

Day 3 ....

Practice Spelling Words

Practice using the Activity Bank.

 **15 minutes**

Day 4 ....

Review Spelling Words

Review using the online activity.

Offline ⏱ 15 minutes

Day 5

Unit Checkpoint

1. **Dictate** the Heart Words and Target Words.

2. **Check** students' answers.

3. **Review** the words students misspelled.

Rewards:

- If students scored 80 percent or above on the Unit Checkpoint, add a sticker to the Unit 32 box on students' My Accomplishments chart. If students scored under 80 percent, continue to practice the words that they missed and add a sticker to this unit once they have mastered the words.

- Help students find and play the online Spelling game, Spell 'n' Stack. Students should use levels 1 and 2.

Heart Words and Consonant Suffixes (B)

Target spelling convention — **words ending in** *–ly, –ment, –ness, –ful,* **or** *–less*

Consonant suffixes do not usually change the spelling of base words. However, when a base word ends in *y,* we usually change the *y* to an *i* when we add the consonant suffixes *–ly, –ment, –ness, –ful,* or *–less.* Each of this unit's Target Words contains a base word that has had one of these consonant suffixes added.

Objectives
- Spell Heart Words.
- Spell words ending in the consonant suffixes *–ly, –ment, –ness, –ful,* or *–less.*

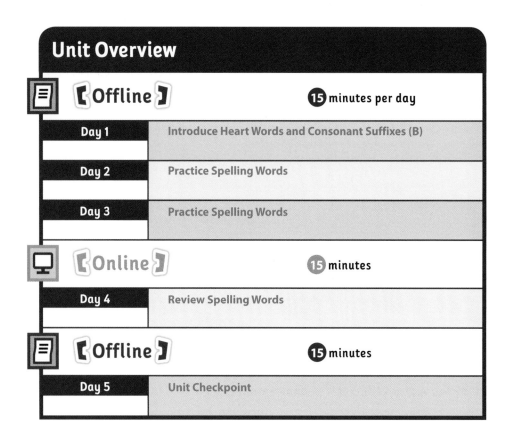

Unit Overview

Offline 15 minutes per day

Day 1	Introduce Heart Words and Consonant Suffixes (B)
Day 2	Practice Spelling Words
Day 3	Practice Spelling Words

Online 15 minutes

| Day 4 | Review Spelling Words |

Offline 15 minutes

| Day 5 | Unit Checkpoint |

Heart Words

floor   listen   whole

Challenge Words

thoughtless   entertainment   awesomeness

Target Words

completely	replacement	priceless
extremely	happiness	actively
politely	spoonful	respectful
settlement		

Alternate Words

secretly	evenly	lively
happily	politeness	refreshment
completeness	placement	powerful
dreadful		

[Offline] 🕐 minutes per day

Complete the Spelling activities with students. **For the full instructions for each activity, refer to pages SP 8–13.**

Day 1 ....

Introduce Heart Words and Consonant Suffixes (B)

[Materials]

- index cards (26)
- whiteboard (optional)

Advance Preparation

Write each Heart, Target, Challenge, and Alternate Word on a separate index card. Indicate on each card whether a word is a Heart, Target, Challenge, or Alternate Word.

Pretest

1. **Administer** a pretest using the Heart and Target Words.

2. **Gather** students' Words to Learn cards.

Note: If students didn't misspell any Heart, Target, Challenge, or Alternate Words, mark Lessons 2 and 3 complete and move to the online activity for Day 4 to practice for the Unit Checkpoint on Day 5.

Heart Words

➲ *Skip this activity if students didn't misspell any Heart Words on this unit's pretest.*

1. **Gather** the Words to Learn cards for any Heart Words.

2. **Practice** the *new* Heart Words.

3. **Practice** *all* Heart Words.

4. **Track mastery** of Heart Words.

Target Words

➲ *Skip this activity if students didn't misspell any Target Words on this unit's pretest.*

1. **Gather** the Words to Learn cards for any Target Words.

2. **Discover** the new spelling convention.

3. **Practice** the Target Words.

Challenge Words

↪ *Skip this activity if students are struggling with the Heart Words and Target Words.*

1. **Gather** the Words to Learn cards for any Challenge Words.
2. **Discover** the new spelling convention in the Challenge Words.
3. **Practice** the Challenge Words.

Alternate Words

↪ *Skip this activity if students don't have any Words to Learn cards for Alternate Words.*

1. **Gather** the Words to Learn cards for any Alternate Words.
2. **Discover** the new spelling convention in the Alternate Words.
3. **Practice** the Alternate Words.

Day 2 ....

Practice Spelling Words

Practice using the Activity Bank.

Day 3 ....

Practice Spelling Words

Practice using the Activity Bank.

 **15** minutes

Day 4 ....

Review Spelling Words

Review using the online activity.

Day 5

Unit Checkpoint

1. **Dictate** the Heart Words and Target Words.

2. **Check** students' answers.

3. **Review** the words students misspelled.

 Rewards:

- If students scored 80 percent or above on the Unit Checkpoint, add a sticker to the Unit 33 box on students' My Accomplishments chart. If students scored under 80 percent, continue to practice the words that they missed and add a sticker to this unit once they have mastered the words.

- Help students find and play the online Spelling game, Spell 'n' Stack. Students should use levels 1 and 2.

Heart Words and Unusual Plurals

Target spelling convention – *f* to *v* + *es* plurals; consonant-*o* + *es* plurals; unchanged plurals; unique plurals

To make some words that end in *f* plural, we change the *f* to a *v* and add *es*. To make some words that end in a consonant and then the letter *o* plural, we add *es*. Some words, such as *sheep* and *deer*, do not change when they are made plural. Other plurals, such as *feet* and *teeth*, must be memorized. Each of this unit's Target Words is an unusual plural.

Objectives
- Spell Heart Words.
- Spell words with unusual plurals.

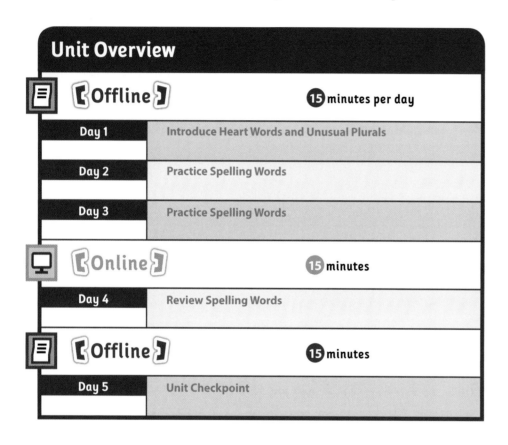

Unit Overview

Offline — 15 minutes per day

Day 1	Introduce Heart Words and Unusual Plurals
Day 2	Practice Spelling Words
Day 3	Practice Spelling Words

Online — 15 minutes

| Day 4 | Review Spelling Words |

Offline — 15 minutes

| Day 5 | Unit Checkpoint |

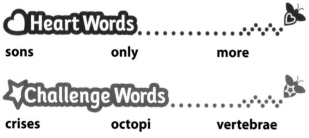

Heart Words

sons   only   more

Challenge Words

crises   octopi   vertebrae

Target Words

calves	mice	sheep
leaves	teeth	deer
feet	children	tornadoes
geese		

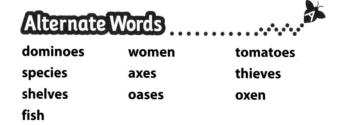

Alternate Words

dominoes	women	tomatoes
species	axes	thieves
shelves	oases	oxen
fish		

[Offline] ⓯ minutes per day

Complete the Spelling activities with students. **For the full instructions for each activity, refer to pages SP 8–13.**

Day 1 ....

Introduce Heart Words and Unusual Plurals

Advance Preparation

Write each Heart, Target, Challenge, and Alternate Word on a separate index card. Indicate on each card whether a word is a Heart, Target, Challenge, or Alternate Word.

Pretest

1. **Administer** a pretest using the Heart and Target Words.

2. **Gather** students' Words to Learn cards.

Note: If students didn't misspell any Heart, Target, Challenge, or Alternate Words, mark Lessons 2 and 3 complete and move to the online activity for Day 4 to practice for the Unit Checkpoint on Day 5.

Heart Words

⮑ *Skip this activity if students didn't misspell any Heart Words on this unit's pretest.*

1. **Gather** the Words to Learn cards for any Heart Words.

2. **Practice** the *new* Heart Words.

3. **Practice** *all* Heart Words.

4. **Track mastery** of Heart Words.

Target Words

⮑ *Skip this activity if students didn't misspell any Target Words on this unit's pretest.*

1. **Gather** the Words to Learn cards for any Target Words.

2. **Discover** the new spelling convention.

3. **Practice** the Target Words.

Challenge Words

➲ *Skip this activity if students are struggling with the Heart Words and Target Words.*

1. **Gather** the Words to Learn cards for any Challenge Words.
2. **Discover** the new spelling convention in the Challenge Words.
3. **Practice** the Challenge Words.

Alternate Words

➲ *Skip this activity if students don't have any Words to Learn cards for Alternate Words.*

1. **Gather** the Words to Learn cards for any Alternate Words.
2. **Discover** the new spelling convention in the Alternate Words.
3. **Practice** the Alternate Words.

Day 2

Practice Spelling Words

Practice using the Activity Bank.

Day 3

Practice Spelling Words

Practice using the Activity Bank.

 **15 minutes**

Day 4

Review Spelling Words

Review using the online activity.

[Offline] 15 minutes

Unit Checkpoint

1. **Dictate** the Heart Words and Target Words.

2. **Check** students' answers.

3. **Review** the words students misspelled.

Rewards:

- If students scored 80 percent or above on the Unit Checkpoint, add a sticker to the Unit 34 box on students' My Accomplishments chart. If students scored under 80 percent, continue to practice the words that they missed and add a sticker to this unit once they have mastered the words.

- Help students find and play the online Spelling game, Spell 'n' Stack. Students should use levels 1 and 2.

Heart Words and Silent Consonants in the Pairs *wr–*, *–mb*, & *kn–*

Target spelling convention – **silent consonants within common consonant pairs**

Some consonant pairs have a silent consonant. In the pair *wr–*, the *w* is silent, as in *wrap*. In the pair *–mb*, the *b* is silent, as in *lamb*. In the pair *kn–*, the *k* is silent, as in *know*. This unit's Target Words all contain a consonant pair with a silent consonant.

Objectives
- Spell Heart Words.
- Spell words containing silent consonants in the pairs *wr–*, *–mb*, and *kn–*.

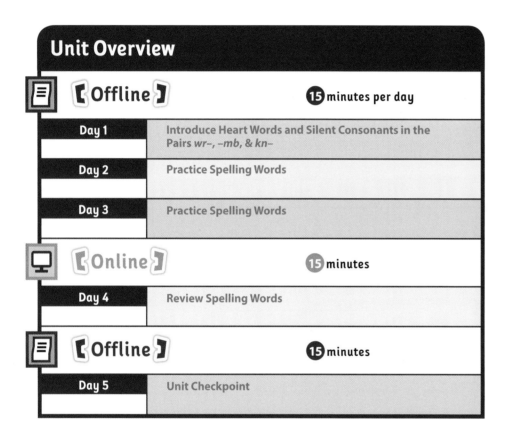

Unit Overview

📝	**〔Offline〕**	⏱15 minutes per day
Day 1	Introduce Heart Words and Silent Consonants in the Pairs *wr–*, *–mb*, & *kn–*	
Day 2	Practice Spelling Words	
Day 3	Practice Spelling Words	

🖥	**〔Online〕**	⏱15 minutes
Day 4	Review Spelling Words	

📝	**〔Offline〕**	⏱15 minutes
Day 5	Unit Checkpoint	

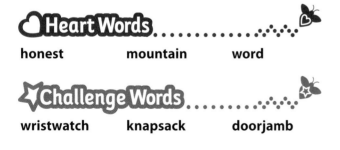

♡ Heart Words

honest	mountain	word

☆ Challenge Words

wristwatch	knapsack	doorjamb

◎ Target Words

write	comb	know
wreath	thumb	knife
wrist	lamb	knee
wrong		

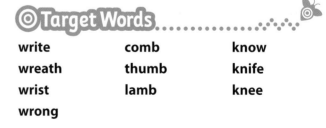

Alternate Words

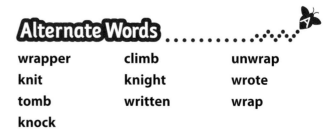

wrapper	climb	unwrap
knit	knight	wrote
tomb	written	wrap
knock		

【Offline 】 ⏱ 15 minutes per day

Complete the Spelling activities with students. **For the full instructions for each activity, refer to pages SP 8–13.**

Day 1

Introduce Heart Words and Silent Consonants in the Pairs *wr–*, *–mb*, & *kn–*

Materials

- index cards (26)
- whiteboard (optional)

Advance Preparation

Write each Heart, Target, Challenge, and Alternate Word on a separate index card. Indicate on each card whether a word is a Challenge or Alternate Word.

Pretest

1. **Administer** a pretest using the Heart and Target Words.

2. **Gather** students' Words to Learn cards.

Note: If students didn't misspell any Heart, Target, Challenge, or Alternate Words, mark Lessons 2 and 3 complete and move to the online activity for Day 4 to practice for the Unit Checkpoint on Day 5.

Heart Words

➲ *Skip this activity if students didn't misspell any Heart Words on this unit's pretest.*

1. **Gather** the Words to Learn cards for any Heart Words.

2. **Practice** the *new* Heart Words.

3. **Practice** *all* Heart Words.

4. **Track mastery** of Heart Words.

Target Words

➲ *Skip this activity if students didn't misspell any Target Words on this unit's pretest.*

1. **Gather** the Words to Learn cards for any Target Words.

2. **Discover** the new spelling convention.

3. **Practice** the Target Words.

Challenge Words

➲ *Skip this activity if students are struggling with the Heart Words and Target Words.*

1. **Gather** the Words to Learn cards for any Challenge Words.
2. **Discover** the new spelling convention in the Challenge Words.
3. **Practice** the Challenge Words.

Alternate Words

➲ *Skip this activity if students don't have any Words to Learn cards for Alternate Words.*

1. **Gather** the Words to Learn cards for any Alternate Words.
2. **Discover** the new spelling convention in the Alternate Words.
3. **Practice** the Alternate Words.

Day 2 ....

Practice Spelling Words

Practice using the Activity Bank.

Day 3 ....

Practice Spelling Words

Practice using the Activity Bank.

 **15 minutes**

Day 4 ....

Review Spelling Words

Review using the online activity.

[Offline] 🕐 **15** minutes

Day 5

Unit Checkpoint

1. **Dictate** the Heart Words and Target Words.

2. **Check** students' answers.

3. **Review** the words students misspelled.

Rewards:

- If students scored 80 percent or above on the Unit Checkpoint, add a sticker to the Unit 35 box on students' My Accomplishments chart. If students scored under 80 percent, continue to practice the words that they missed and add a sticker to this unit once they have mastered the words.

- Help students find and play the online Spelling game, Spell 'n' Stack. Students should use levels 1 and 2.

Review Heart Words, Syllables, Suffixes, Unusual Plurals, and Silent Consonants

In this unit, students will review the spelling conventions and Heart Words they studied in the previous five units. Refer back to the Unit Plans of previous units for a detailed description of each spelling convention.

Objectives

- Spell Heart Words.
- Spell multisyllabic words containing vowel-team syllables.
- Spell words ending with the vowel suffixes *–ed*, *–est*, *–ing*, or *–er*.
- Spell words requiring a doubled consonant before the endings *–ed* or *–ing*.
- Spell words ending in the consonant suffixes *–ly*, *–ment*, *–ness*, *–ful*, or *–less*.
- Spell words with unusual plurals.
- Spell words containing silent consonants in the pairs *wr–*, *–mb*, and *kn–*.

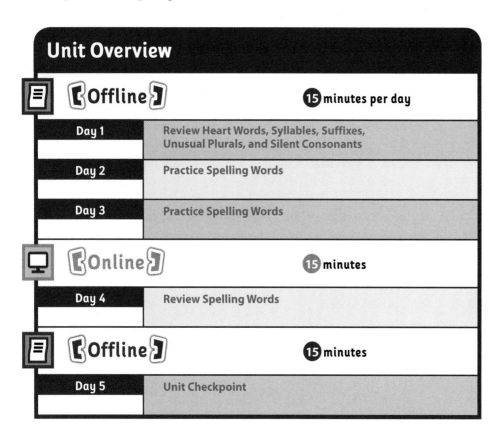

Unit Overview

📋 **[Offline]** — 🕐 15 minutes per day

Day 1	Review Heart Words, Syllables, Suffixes, Unusual Plurals, and Silent Consonants
Day 2	Practice Spelling Words
Day 3	Practice Spelling Words

💻 **[Online]** — 🕐 15 minutes

Day 4	Review Spelling Words

📋 **[Offline]** — 🕐 15 minutes

Day 5	Unit Checkpoint

☁ Heart Words

journey	always	only
flood	floor	more
calf	listen	honest
door	whole	mountain
talk	sons	word

★ Challenge Words

loneliness	cacti	wrongful

◎ Target Words

railroad	nicest	teeth
fifteen	politely	write
display	respectful	lamb
tapping	leaves	knee

Alternate Words

painful	fulfillment	knack
taped	potatoes	

Offline ⏱ **15 minutes per day**

Complete the Spelling activities with students. **For the full instructions for each activity, refer to pages SP 8–13.**

Day 1

Review Heart Words, Syllables, Suffixes, Unusual Plurals, and Silent Consonants

 **Materials**

- index cards (8)
- whiteboard (optional)

Advance Preparation

Gather the index cards you made previously for the Heart and Target Words listed. Write each Challenge and Alternate Word on a separate index card. Indicate on each card whether a word is a Challenge or Alternate Word.

Pretest

1. **Administer** a pretest using the Heart and Target Words.

2. **Gather** students' Words to Learn cards.

Note: If students didn't misspell any Heart, Target, Challenge, or Alternate Words, mark Lessons 2 and 3 complete and move to the online activity for Day 4 to practice for the Unit Checkpoint on Day 5.

Heart Words

➲ *Skip this activity if students didn't misspell any Heart Words on this unit's pretest.*

1. **Gather** the Words to Learn cards for any Heart Words.

2. **Practice** the Heart Words.

3. **Track mastery** of Heart Words.

Target Words

➲ *Skip this activity if students didn't misspell any Target Words on this unit's pretest.*

1. **Gather** the Words to Learn cards for any Target Words.

2. **Review** the previously studied spelling convention in each Target Word.

3. **Practice** the Target Words.

Challenge Words

⮑ *Skip this activity if students are struggling with the Heart Words and Target Words.*

1. **Gather** the Words to Learn cards for any Challenge Words.
2. **Review** the previously studied spelling convention in each Challenge Word.
3. **Practice** the Challenge Words.

Alternate Words

⮑ *Skip this activity if students don't have any Words to Learn cards for Alternate Words.*

1. **Gather** the Words to Learn cards for any Alternate Words.
2. **Review** the previously studied spelling convention in each Alternate Word.
3. **Practice** the Alternate Words.

Day 2 ....

Practice Spelling Words

Practice using the Activity Bank.

Day 3 ....

Practice Spelling Words

Practice using the Activity Bank.

 **minutes**

Day 4 ....

Review Spelling Words

Review using the online activity.

〔 Offline 〕 ⏱ **15** minutes

Unit Checkpoint

1. **Dictate** the Heart Words and Target Words.

2. **Check** students' answers.

3. **Review** the words students misspelled.

Rewards:

- If students scored 80 percent or above on the Unit Checkpoint, add a sticker to the Unit 36 box on students' My Accomplishments chart. If students scored under 80 percent, continue to practice the words that they missed and add a sticker to this unit once they have mastered the words.

- Help students find and play the online Spelling game, Spell 'n' Stack. Students should use levels 1 and 2.

Spelling Activity Bank

Word Train

1. Say each of the Words to Learn to students.

2. Ask students to write each word end-to-end as one long word, using different colors of crayon or ink for different words.

3. Note any words that students spelled incorrectly, and correct the spelling errors with students.

Vowel-Free Words

1. Say each of the Words to Learn to students. Have students write only the consonants in the word and put a dot where each vowel belongs.

2. Have students tell you which vowel belongs where they placed each dot.

3. Note any words that students spelled incorrectly, and correct the spelling errors with students.

Spelling Memory

1. Ask students to write as many of the Words to Learn as they can remember on a sheet of paper.

2. When students finish, remind them of any words they forgot and have them complete the list.

3. Note any words that students spelled incorrectly, and correct the spelling errors with students.

Fill In the Blank

1. Write a sentence that uses one of the Words to Learn, but leave a blank space where that word would go in the sentence.

2. Ask students to fill in the word that completes the sentence. Sometimes more than one word will correctly complete a sentence.

3. Repeat with each of the Words to Learn.

4. Note any words that students spelled incorrectly, and correct the spelling errors with students.

Silly Sentences

1. Ask students to write a silly sentence using each of the Words to Learn.

2. Have students underline the spelling word in each sentence.

3. Note any words that students spelled incorrectly, and correct the spelling errors with students.

Sample sentence

The dog was driving a car.

Spelling Baseball

1. Draw a baseball diamond with four bases (see example).

2. Tell students that you are the pitcher and they are the batters.

3. Choose a word from the Words to Learn and ask students to spell it.

   ▸ If students spell the word correctly, they get to move one base.
   ▸ If students spell the word incorrectly, that is one strike.
   ▸ If students get three strikes on the same word, that is one out.
   ▸ If students spell four words correctly, they have moved around all four bases. They score a run (one point)!

4. Continue giving students words until each of the Words to Learn has been used. See how many points students can earn.

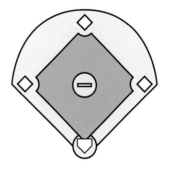

Spelling Story

Have students write a very short story using as many of the Words to Learn as they can.

Which Is Correct?

1. Write out three versions of one of the Words to Learn, spelling two versions incorrectly and one correctly.

2. Say the word.

3. Have students pick out which of the versions is correct and write the correct spelling of the word.

Alphabetize

1. Have students write the Words to Learn in alphabetical order.

2. Note any words that students spelled incorrectly, and correct the spelling errors with students.

Word Pyramids

Have students write each of the Words to Learn in a word pyramid. Be sure that students write neatly so that the pyramid shape can be seen.

```
        p
      p   a
    p   a   s
  p   a   s   s
```

Guess the Word

1. Say any letter from one of the Words to Learn. Ask students to guess which word you are thinking of.

2. Say a second letter in the word, a third, and so on until students correctly guess your word.

3. After students guess the word, have them spell that word aloud.

4. Repeat the activity with several words.

Guess the Word Reversed

1. Have students say any letter from one of the Words to Learn. Try to guess which word students are thinking of.

2. Have students say a second letter in the word, a third, and so on until you're able to correctly guess their word.

3. After you guess the word, have students spell that word aloud.

4. Repeat the activity with several words.

Hidden Picture

1. Have students draw a picture and "hide" as many of the Words to Learn as they can inside the picture.

2. See if you or others can find the words within the picture. (The example picture has the words *can, fix, fun,* and *red* hidden in it.)

3. Note any words that students spelled incorrectly, and correct the spelling errors with students.

Word Scramble

1. Write the letters of each of the Words to Learn in scrambled order.

2. Have students write the correctly spelled word next to each of your scrambled words.

Spelling Scene

Have students draw a picture representing as many of the Words to Learn as they can. Students should label the picture with the spelling words.

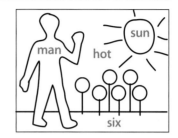

Rhymes

1. Have students write each of the Words to Learn.

2. Next to each word, have them write a rhyming word.

3. If there is time, have students try to come up with more than one rhyming word for some of the Words to Learn.

TIP Students may come across rhyming words that are from different word families and are spelled with different spelling conventions (such as *half* and *laugh*). These rhymes are valid, but discuss the differences in spellings with students.

Rhymes Reversed

1. For each of the Words to Learn, write a word that rhymes with it on a sheet of paper and then leave a space blank.

2. In the blank, have students fill in the word that rhymes with the word you wrote.

3. Note any words that students spelled incorrectly, and correct the spelling errors with students.

TIP Do not include rhyming words that are from different word families and are spelled with different spelling conventions (such as *half* and *laugh*). These rhymes are valid, but the differences in spelling can be confusing to students.

Crosswords

1. Have students write one of the Words to Learn vertically in the center of a sheet of paper.

2. Have them write another of the Words to Learn by going across and sharing a letter with the first word.

3. See how many words students can connect.

```
                          p
                k  i  s  s  e  s
             d     n
          r  o  c  k  s
             g
```

Roll the Number Cube

1. Have students roll the number cube.

2. Have students write the one of the Words to Learn the number of times indicated by their roll.

3. Continue the process, having students roll the cube and write a word that many times, until they've written all the Words to Learn.

4. Note any words that students spelled incorrectly, and correct the spelling errors with students.

Materials

- household objects –
  six-sided number cube
  (labeled 1 through 6)

Snowman

1. Draw a snowman with three circles for the body and head, two eyes, a nose, and hands (see example).

2. Pick one of the Words to Learn, but do not tell students which word you have chosen.

3. Draw one blank space under the snowman for each letter of the word.

4. Ask students to guess what letters might be in the word you have chosen.

5. Each time students make an incorrect guess, erase one part of the snowman. The object of the game is for students to try to guess the whole word before the snowman melts.

Finger Spelling

1. With students turned away from you, tell them you will be spelling one of the Words to Learn on their back with your finger.

2. Using one finger, trace each letter of one of the Words to Learn on the back of a student. Ask the student to guess what word you are spelling.

3. To extend the activity, have students take a turn spelling words on your back.

Spelling Search

1. Have students search for the Words to Learn in newspapers, books, or magazines.

2. Have them write down each word as they find it.

Materials

- household objects (optional) – newspaper, book, magazine

Word Search Puzzle

1. Draw a large box on a sheet of lined paper or graph paper.

2. Fill in the box with Words to Learn, writing them horizontally, vertically, and diagonally (forward or backward if you choose).

3. Fill in the rest of the box with random letters.

4. Have students find and circle the Words to Learn in the puzzle.

Quickfire

1. Tell students to write down each word you say as quickly as they can. Warn them, however, that misspellings come with a ten-second penalty.

2. Then time how long it takes students to write all of the Words to Learn after you say them.

3. Check their list for misspellings, tacking on ten seconds for each mistake.

4. Encourage students to try again and improve their time.

5. After two or more attempts, note any words that students spelled incorrectly, and correct the spelling errors with students.

Materials

- household objects – watch with a second hand

Pictionary/Charades

1. Draw or act out something to make students guess one of the Words to Learn.

2. When students guess correctly, have them write down the word.

3. Repeat the activity with several words.

4. Note any words that students spelled incorrectly, and correct the spelling errors with students.

Mnemonics

1. Have students write one of the Words to Learn vertically. Check make sure they have spelled the word correctly.

2. Then have them write words horizontally that begin with each letter of the vertical word.

3. Encourage students to say the vertical word, then the horizontal words, and then the vertical word again.

w	e			
a	l	l		to
l	o	v	e	
k	i	t	e	s

Mnemonics Reversed

1. Come up with a mnemonic for one of the Words to Learn.

2. Say the mnemonic for students. Explain that the first letter of each word you said combine to spell a word from this unit.

3. Then have students say and spell the Word to Learn based on your mnemonic.

4. Note any words that students spelled incorrectly, and correct the spelling errors with students.

Example	**walk**
You say	**"we all love kites"**
Students write	**"w-a-l-k"**

Right or Wrong?

1. Tell students that you are going to spell one of the Words to Learn.

2. Explain that their job is to listen and decide whether your spelling is right or wrong.

3. After you spell each word, check with students for their verdict. If your spelling was incorrect, have students spell the word correctly.

Eat Your Words

1. Give students a bag of thin pretzel sticks.

2. Explain that their job is to listen to the words you say, and then use the pretzel sticks to make the letters that spell each word.

3. Say each of the Words to Learn.

4. After students create each word, check their spelling.